Martin Loney is senior lecturer in social policy and head of inter-disciplinary social sciences at the Open University. He was formerly General Secretary of the National Council for Civil Liberties and International Research Director for World University Service in Geneva. He has taught at the South Bank Polytechnic, London and at Carleton University, Canada. His previous publications include *Rhodesia: White Racism and Imperial Response* (Penguin 1975) and *Community Against Government* (Heinemann 1983). He was editor of *The Crisis of the Inner City* (Macmillan 1979) and *Social Policy and Social Welfare* (Open University Press 1983). His articles have appeared in *The Times Higher Education Supplement*, *The Times Educational Supplement* and *Tribune*. He is a regular contributor to the magazine *Community Care*. A former Labour County Council candidate in rural Bedfordshire, the author succeeded in doubling the size of the Labour vote and bringing them in a magnificent third.

Martin Loney

The Politics of Greed

The New Right and the Welfare State

Pluto  Press

London   Sydney   Dover New Hampshire

First published in 1986 by Pluto Press Limited,
The Works, 105a Torriano Avenue, London NW5 2RX
and Pluto Press Australia Limited, PO Box 199, Leichhardt,
New South Wales 2040, Australia. Also Pluto Press,
51 Washington Street, Dover, New Hampshire 03820, USA

7 6 5 4 3 2 1

90 89 88 87 86

Set by Boldface Typesetters, London EC1
Printed in Great Britain by Guernsey Press Co. Ltd.
Guernsey, C.I.

British Library Cataloguing in Publication Data
Loney, Martin
   The politics of greed: the new right and the
   Welfare State.
   1. Great Britain – Social policy   2. Great
   Britain – Politics and government – 1979-
   I. Title
   361.6'1'0941   HN390

ISBN 0 7453 0145 2

Contents

Acknowledgements

Thanks are due to Wendy Lloyd and Tony Fitzgerald for research assistance, and to Carol Johns, whose proficiency with the typescript improved both the speed and quality of production. Allan Cochrane and John Clarke made useful comments on the manuscript.

If you believe economic salvation can only be achieved by rewarding success and the national income is not increasing, then you have no alternative but to make the unsuccessful poorer. (Reg Prentice, Social Security Minister, 1979)

What is it that impels the powerful and vocal lobby in Britain to press for greater equality . . . Often the reasons boil down to an undistinguished combination of envy and what might be termed 'bourgeois guilt'. (Margaret Thatcher, 1975)

Giving money to Liverpool is rather like sending food to Ethiopia . . . Unemployment in Liverpool, like famine in Africa, is almost entirely caused by human folly and wickedness. (Richard West in the *Spectator*, April 1983)

Society rightly feels that elderly parents and relatives for example . . . are the responsibility of next-of-kin to help. The same is true of handicapped children . . . Neglect of these family responsibilities would be actionable by the state . . . Social services would be necessary, just as police are necessary to maintain law and order. (Patrick Minford, 1984)

The truth is, as history has so often shown us, that unfettered market forces lead to the rich and the strong growing richer and stronger and the poor and the weak, poorer and weaker until some conflagration in society acted to restore the balance. (Edward Heath, 1985)

Introduction

The election of the Thatcher government in 1979 was widely heralded as marking a decisive shift in public attitudes both towards the proper role of government and more particularly in regard to the merits of the welfare state. In fact it would be quite wrong to draw such conclusions, but what is not open to dispute is that the new government's view of the welfare state stood in marked contrast not only to the rhetoric of the Labour Party but also to much traditional Conservative thinking.

The government's position was rooted in the writings of the ultra-monetarist Institute for Economic Affairs, in the philosophy of Hayek and the economics of Friedman. The commitment to the more arcane reaches of a particular brand of economics stood in marked contrast to the explicitly pragmatic Tory tradition exemplified in Macmillan's dictum: 'Economics and social policy are not a question of dogma but of judgement' (Macmillan, 1966, p. xxvii).

The proclaimed sanctity of the market and a fundamental hostility to the welfare state went hand in hand with an explicit commitment to increasing income differentials. Incentives and self-reliance were the domestic code words of the new Conservatism. Incentives were to operate for the poor and the rich. For the rich, lower taxation was to produce a prodigious increase in effort, whilst for the poor any failure in effort would result in dependency on increasingly meagre state benefits. Lord Kaldor offered an apt analogy for the first part of this equation as a viable explanation for the acknowledged failure of Britain's top management:

We admit that at Passchendaele or in the Battle of the Somme in the First War, the Generals were not at their best — as our historians now say — but please do not believe that this is due to a lack of their innate ability, or to the system of selection. The Generals were slacking in not giving their best because they did not receive sufficient material rewards. (Lord Kaldor, 1983, p. 14)*

No doubt if only British Leyland had paid its managers more and the government had taxed them less, Leyland cars would have been more competitive and nationalization might have been avoided.

Rhoyes Boyson, Social Security Minister in the second Thatcher government, had summarized the broader critique of the welfare state in a book appropriately entitled *Down with the Poor*:

The moral fibre of our people has been weakened. The State which does for its citizens what they can do for themselves is an evil state; and a state which removes all choice and responsibility from its people and makes them like broiler hens will create the irresponsible society. No-one cares, no-one saves, no-one bothers – why should they when the state spends all its energies taking money from the energetic, successful and thrifty to give to the idle, the failures and the feckless? (Boyson, 1971, p. 5)

The stridency of the new right was in marked contrast to the explicit commitment to 'the middle way' of an earlier generation which had claimed the right to govern not least because of a balanced ambivalence:

We do not stand and have never stood for collectivism or the destruction of private rights. We do not stand and have never stood for laissez-faire individualism or for putting the rights of the individual above his duty to his fellow men. We stand today, as we have always stood, to block the way to both these extremes and to all such extremes, and to point the path towards moderate and balanced views. (Macmillan, 1966, p. xxii)

In this book we outline the emergence of the new right to a position of dominance in the Conservative Party, and note the transformation of yesterday's iconoclasts into the architects of

* Full details for the sources of all quotes are given in the bibliography.

the new orthodoxy. We examine the basic propositions of the free marketeers and compare these with other attempts to provide a philosophical and ideological basis for a distinctive right-of-centre Conservatism.

There is an immense gap between the articulation of the pristine texts of political principle and the discovery and exegesis of supposed economic laws, and the day-to-day reality of politics. The difficulty is not simply that the world frequently refuses to respond in the ways imagined and defined, but also that the pressures of party, electorate and a hundred and one unexpected events may contrive to thwart the commitment politician. It may also be the case that commitment politicians grasp only the generalities of ideas which then serve to create the illusion of ideological coherence and the chimera of destiny with which to rally the faithful and as many of the electorate as possible.

There is then the world of ideas, with a presumed logical consistency, whatever the absurdity of the underlying assumptions or the grossness of the possible outcome, and the world of action. In examining the new right and social policy we are inevitably drawn to both; to the idealistic claims of unparalleled prosperity for those who shake themselves free of the weight of the state, the burden of taxation, the barriers to enterprise and so on, and also to the realities of life when Victorian virtues are imposed on the inner-city unemployed. We are also drawn to examine the appeal of the philosophies of the right and ask whether this lies in their intellectual coherence, the quality of their arguments and the strength of the evidence amassed or rather in the ability to mobilize opinion in defence of privilege and to legitimate widening inequalities: a shift in direction which has brought enormous gains to the rich and a parallel increase in both the numbers of the poor and their impoverishment.

1. Architects of the New Right

> The welfare state has gradually changed from the expression of compassion to an instrument of political repression unequalled in British history. (Harris and Seldon, p. 204)

The prominence of the new right in Britain is of relatively recent origin but in the United States it has long played a more influential role. The absence of any strong socialist movement or any equivalent to the British Fabian tradition, together with the strength of the American free enterprise ideology, offered the new right a particularly fertile ground. Indeed, scepticism about government efficiency, attacks on extravagant welfare programmes and assertions of the supreme importance of the individual often seem no more than a restatement of the mainstream American credo.

The American new right, no less than the British, are a somewhat eclectic combination; they include those who deify the market as well as those sceptical of the uncluttered pursuit of materialism. They encompass powerful constituencies of the religiously inspired 'moral majority' eager to ensure that their imagined majority claims are transformed into a universal, legally sanctioned code of behaviour, and libertarians who see in the unfettered operation of the market, and the minimal state, guarantees of wider freedom. It is this diversity of opinion which enables the astute politician to avoid the pitfalls of blind faith while holding true to the wider church. If it is difficult to find in Friedman a rationale for censorship it is always possible to turn to Irving Kristol (Kristol, 1973).

If Hayek has little to say on the appropriate roles for women or the importance of genes in determining achievement, the President in search of support for his prejudices could always turn to the apostles of sociobiology, to a Gilder or a Jensen (Gilder, 1973; Jensen, 1969)

Freedom through the market

> I would guess that Hayek's *Constitution of Liberty* and the
> three volumes of *Law, Legislation and Liberty* have been the
> most influential books behind the present leadership. (Lord
> Thomas, Chairman of the Centre for Policy Studies)

The most important of the early postwar critics of the perceived
trend towards collectivism was Fredrick Von Hayek, author of
The Road to Serfdom, published in 1944. Hayek challenged the
growing role of the state and egalitarian attempts to regulate
social life and asserted the pre-eminence of the individual. Freedom was not simply to be preferred to equality. It was incompat-
ible with it. State provision of a minimum level of income might
be an acceptable guarantee of security, as might state intervention to ensure an adequate system of social insurance. In the
nature of his work Hayek was not concerned with the detail of
social policy but rather with principle. Nonetheless, it was clear
that any specified minimum income would be concerned with
subsistence needs and Hayek explicitly excluded any relative
notion of poverty as a suitable basis for state intervention:

> These two kinds of security are, first, security against severe
> physical privation, the certainty of a given minimum of susten-
> ance for all; and, secondly, the security of a given standard of
> life, or of the relative position which one person or group
> enjoys compared with others ... We shall presently see that
> this distinction largely coincides with the distinction between
> the security which can be provided for all outside of and sup-
> plementary to the market system, and the security which can
> be provided only for some and only by controlling or abolish-
> ing the market. (Hayek, 1944, p. 89)

Hayek's starting point is the individual, and the centrality of
the market is crucial to his argument. For Hayek the erosion of
the unqualified right of the individual to buy and sell in the
market is no less than the gradual extinction of freedom.
Attempts to protect individuals against the vagaries and apparent
injustices which occur in the marketplace or to impose some non-
market criteria of just remuneration must be resisted. Forty years
later Hayek argued, 'The great illusion is that freedom and just

distribution can be combined' (Hayek, 1983). His opposition to
the expanding role of government is succinctly summarized in his
later publication, *Law, Legislation and Liberty*.

Hayek argues that governments have sought and obtained
powers which they were never intended to have by those who conceived the constitution:

> Constitutionalism means limited government. But the inter-
> pretation given to the traditional formulae of constitutional-
> ism has made it possible to reconcile these with a conception of
> democracy according to which this is a form of government
> where the will of the majority on any particular matter is
> unlimited. (Hayek, 1973, p. 1)

Hayek articulates this concern with what he perceives to be the
ever-increasing growth of the state in the form of what he calls 'a
fundamental insight':

> ... the predominant model of liberal democratic institutions,
> in which the same representative body lays down the rules of
> just conduct and directs government, necessarily leads to a
> gradual transformation of the spontaneous order of free society
> into a totalitarian system conducted in the service of some coa-
> lition of organized interests. (*ibid.*, p. 2)

The market is the only alternative to an ultimately totalitarian
direction of individual activity and any talk of imposing criteria
relating to social justice onto the outcomes of the market is misconceived:

> ... the market allocates command over goods and services to
> particular people: this can be neither just nor unjust, because
> the results are not intended or foreseen, and depend on a mul-
> titude of circumstances ... It is the only procedure yet discov-
> ered in which information widely dispersed among millions of
> men can be effectively utilized for the benefit of all – and used
> by assuring to all an individual liberty desirable for itself on
> ethical grounds ... It is a procedure which, as Adam Smith ...
> understood in all important respects is wholly analogous to a
> game ... with the consequence that the outcome will be unpre-
> dictable and that there will regularly be winners and losers.
> (Hayek, 1976, pp. 70 and 71)

Hayek not only dismisses the notion of social justice as misconceived and ultimately without content (*ibid.*, p. xii) he also rejects the possibility of equality of opportunity:

> To achieve this, government would have to control the whole physical and human environment of all persons, and have to endeavour to provide at least equivalent chances for each; and the more government succeeded in these endeavours, the stronger would become the legitimate demands that, on the same principle, any still remaining handicaps must be removed – or compensated for by putting extra burden on the still relatively favoured. This would have to go on until government literally controlled every circumstance which could affect any person's wellbeing. (*ibid.*, pp. 84 and 85)

Here, as elsewhere, Hayek claims an inexorable progression from limited intervention, in pursuit of broad goals, to ultimate tyranny.

There are a number of difficulties with Hayek's argument. Markets in advanced industrial societies do not operate in the unregulated and even random way which Hayek suggests. The concentration of economic power in the hands of a decreasing number of multinational corporations concerned to control and increase market shares and the interpenetration of government and private sector industry are two obvious counter points. The fortunes of many industries, most notably in the defence field, are closely tied to government policies. Market success is not determined by any abstract principle of competitiveness but often by the purchasing policies of central government and by the close links forged between key individuals who frequently cross from one side to the other. When Mr Peter Levene, Chairman of United Scientific Holdings and Vice-Chairman of the Defence Manufacturers Association, and former political adviser to Defence Secretary Heseltine, was appointed as the Ministry's Chief of Defence Procurement, his position at United Scientific Holdings was taken by the former permanent Secretary at the Ministry of Defence, Sir Frank Cooper (the *Guardian*, 21 December 1984). Galbraith, commenting on the links between defence industries and the defence establishment, argued that in the United States the Pentagon had abandones any effort at controlling the industry: 'by according major authority in the Defence

Department and over the armed services to executives from the weapons firms or their lobbyists. It is not civilian control but rather incestuous administration of the military-industrial complex by the military-industrial complex' (quoted in Johnson, 1984). Yet such close intermeshing of the state and business seems more characteristic of advanced capitalist societies than the picture drawn by Hayek. This is the reality of contemporary advanced capitalism at both the national and international level which Hayek surprisingly ignores.

A more general political problem which Hayek's philosophy raises is why individuals should agree to accept the outcomes of the market, particularly since, as Hayek acknowledges, individuals will not only experience unequal outcomes but will also enter the marketplace with unequal advantages. Those with privileged access may well support market ideologies which serve to legitimate their further success. Companies may seek to restrict competition where it threatens their profits and to encourage government intervention where it furthers their profits while simultaneously advocating the supremacy of market mechanisms. Hayek's proclaimed influence on key Conservative politicians cannot perhaps be divorced from the compatibility between this philosophy and their own backgrounds. It may be that the number of Old Etonians in Conservative cabinets has declined, but the self-made aura with which the modern party seeks to surround itself cannot be taken at face value. The leadership of the party remains in the hands of those who started the race with a considerable advantage or took the precaution of marrying others who did so at the earliest opportunity. They owe their success not to any 'hidden hand' but to the continuing salience of social class and the privileges and disadvantages which it encompasses.

In power the Thatcher government was to demonstrate that commitment to market mechanisms was rather more ambivalent than any philosophy might have suggested. Free-market rhetoric provided a plausible justification for measures to turn over increasing areas of economic activity to the private sector. Behind the rhetoric of competitiveness and efficiency, measures could be taken to depress the wages and working conditions of low-paid sectors of society. The same rhetoric was not directed against more privileged groups who continued to enjoy protected environments. The stock exchange was to be left to regulate itself.

Farmers afloat in a sea of subsidies saw their income significantly increased – in 1982 by no less than 45 per cent. Indeed, it quickly became clear that the Thatcher government was unable in practice to distinguish between measures to turn over state assets to the private sector and measures intended to use the mechanism of market competition to increase the efficiency of particular industries. British Telecom was privatized with considerable advantages to those affluent enough to purchase shares but with no increase whatsoever in the market forces to which British Telecom was to be subject. The company retained its monopoly position and became even less accountable to the public than previously.

It is difficult to envisage a situation in which the kind of unfettered market envisaged by Hayek might operate. In reality, powerful groups will seek to ensure that outcomes are favourable to particular interests. Defence manufacturers will demand and receive from the government rates of return on capital far in excess of those prevalent in the economy as a whole. Drug manufacturers will demand and receive protection from foreign competition. Automobile manufacturers will operate profit maximizing discriminatory pricing policies contrary to the EEC regulations, secure in the knowledge that the nature of the EEC and the power of the automobile industries will make reform both slow and ineffective. Only the weak and the unorganized will feel the unmitigated effects of market mechanisms. School dinner ladies may have their pay cut, their holiday entitlement abolished and even find their jobs disappear over night. The British Oxygen Corporation, in contrast, will find its high earnings from the NHS relatively secure.

Hayek's influence may have been largely indirect in that politicians and commentators were by and large less likely to read the dense and somewhat inaccessible writings of Hayek than the more polemical, policy directed writings of those who are more effective publicists. Hayek's work was, on the other hand, well known amongst more intellectual right-wing Conservatives, including Sir Keith Joseph. Rhodes Boyson has identified Hayek as the key intellectual influence in providing 'the philosophical base' for his views:

His book, *Law, Legislation and Liberty*, published in 1976, is one to which I turn regularly. It outlines the principles on which a free society must be based and how, if these principles are forgotten – even if by good and well-intentioned men and women – the free society will fall and some form of tyranny will triumph. (*Community Care*, 22 December 1983, p. 15)

Even Margaret Thatcher claimed to have been wrestling with the ideas of Hayek for over thirty years, though one commentator politely described this proposition as 'far-fetched' (Keegan, 1984, p. 81)

In praise of money

Milton Friedman has effectively combined the role of academic with that of publicist, commentator and government advisor. His views on the centrality of monetary policy to the control of inflation are widely known, though the evidence for them is under deafening attack. Professor Hendry, a leading econometrician, commented on a study of Friedman's major work in the area: 'One of the most amazing things about our study is that we have not been able to find any evidence that money supply creates either income growth or inflation' (Huhne, 15 December 1983).

Of greater concern here are Friedman's convictions that freedom is only guaranteed by the unfettered operation of a market economy, that government is necessarily a less efficient provider of the vast bulk of goods and services, and that most welfare measures constitute an unjustified burden on society and simultaneously depress economic growth without achieving their objectives. Friedman does not claim that capitalism guarantees freedom, only that it is an essential prerequisite. Since Friedman equates freedom with the activities of the individual in the marketplace and sees no essential difference between infringements of the right to spend one's income without external constraint and other democratic rights, his argument is to some extent tautologous. He cites, for example, the refusal of a group of farmers of the Amish sect to contribute to the federal old-age programmes on grounds of principle:

As a result, some of their livestock were sold by auction in order to satisfy claims for social security levies. True, the number of citizens who regard compulsory old-age insurance as a deprivation of freedom may be few, but the believer in freedom has never counted noses. (Friedman, 1962, p. 9)

For Friedman 'the basic problem of social organization is how to co-ordinate the economic activities of large numbers of people' (*ibid.*, p. 12). This can be resolved either by central direction or via the marketplace. Exchange in the market offers the opportunity for 'co-ordination without coercion' (*ibid.*, p. 13). The operation of the market benefits all participants: 'Each household uses the resources it controls to produce goods and services that it exchanges for goods and services produced by other households, on terms mutually acceptable to the two parties to the bargain' (*ibid.*, p. 13). Friedman recognizes that modern markets contain large enterprises and depend on the use of money but this does not change the essentials:

The central characteristic of the market technique of achieving co-ordination is fully displayed in the simple exchange economy that contains neither enterprises nor money. As in that simple model, so in the complex enterprise and money-exchange economy, co-operation is strictly individual and voluntary provided: (a) that enterprises are private . . . and (b) that individuals are effectively free to enter or not to enter into any particular exchange, so that every transaction is strictly voluntary. (*ibid.*, p. 14)

The market, Friedman claims, minimizes the need for government action and maximizes individual choice whilst simultaneously defending political freedom by offering a diversity of employers, so that even radicals and revolutionaries may find work. The market also serves to counter discrimination:

The existence of a free market does not of course eliminate the need for government . . . government is essential both as a forum for determining the 'rules of the game' and as an umpire . . . What the market does is to reduce greatly the range of issues that must be decided through political means . . . The great advantage of the market . . . is that it permits wide diversity . . . Each man can vote, as it were, for the colour of tie he wants and get it . . . Economic power can be widely dispersed.

There is no law of conservation which forces the growth of
new centres of economic strength to be at the expense of existing centres. Political power . . . is more difficult to decentralize
. . . If economic power is kept in separate hands from political
power, it can serve as a check and a counter to political power.
(*ibid*., pp. 15 and 16)

In support of his argument Friedman cites the ability of social-
ists to raise money, publish newspapers and organize politically
within capitalist societies and the contrasting difficulties that
capitalists would experience in achieving similar political freedom in a socialist society. Individuals may be employed irrespective of their views if for no other reason than that of a desire to
make a profit, a factor which, Friedman argues, ultimately broke
the Hollywood blacklist:

The Hollywood blacklist was an unfree act that destroys freedom because it was a collusive arrangement that used coercive
means to prevent voluntary exchanges. It didn't work precisely
because the market made it costly for people to preserve the
blacklist. The commercial emphasis, the fact that people who
are running enterprises have an incentive to make as much
money as they can, protected the freedom of the individuals
who were blacklisted by providing them with an alternative
form of employment, and by giving people an incentive to
employ them . . . The groups in our society that have the most
at stake in the preservation and strengthening of competitive
capitalism are those minority groups which can most easily
become the object of the distrust and enmity of the majority –
the Negroes, the Jews, the foreign-born to mention only the
most obvious. (*ibid*., pp. 20 and 21)

Friedman is right in pointing to the role of the market and the
institution of private property in creating a viable base for a
genuine plurality of power and opinion. As he notes, such plurality
of power and opinion has not been a characteristic of self-styled
socialist societies. Nonetheless here, as in his general argument
regarding the market, he ignores the increasing concentration of
economic power in fewer and fewer hands. He overlooks the possibility such a harmony of interest and view among these power
holders as to force alternative opinion to the very margins of

society. Indeed, a marked characteristic of western capitalist societies is the strength of groupings in the market which seek to secure or maintain privileged access to the means of communication or indeed to any other resource.

Friedman also asserts that the market protects minority groups. In what Friedman calls an 'ideal free market' (*ibid.*, p. 21) this *may* happen but it is hardly relevant to an understanding of what happens in the real world. In recent years it has been clear that trade unions and employers substantially discriminate against ethnic minority groups and women. Discrimination is not confined to the field of employment, it exists in the provision of goods and services, most notably in the housing field. The remedy to this situation has been sought in government action. An inherent difficulty in Friedman's argument is the assertion that the market is 'impersonal'. In practice it is not. It may be that 'no-one who buys bread knows whether the wheat from which it is made was grown by a Communist or a Republican, by a Constitutionalist or a Fascist, or, for that matter, by a Negro or a white' (*ibid.*, p. 21). However, in practice it is abundantly clear at some point along the road who has grown the wheat and this may very well affect the decision to make a purchase. In the real world prejudice has its own market price and it is not the case, for example, in the field of rented accommodation, that the highest bidder always or even in general wins out. A sufficient number of renters will be prepared to discriminate on the grounds of colour to the extent of taking a lower market price in order to select tenants of the preferred background. Nonetheless, Friedman's faith in the operation of the market is limitless.

> Music or dance, secretarial skills, automobile driving, airplane piloting, technical skills – all are taught best when they are taught privately. Try talking French with someone who had studied it in public (state) school, then with a Berlitz graduate. (quoted in Boyson, 1975, p. 4).

In the circumstances it is indeed remarkable, at least for Friedmanites, that the RAF and USAF have relied on training their own pilots who have then provided a significant pool for recruitment by commercial airlines and not vice versa. But then faith in these matters is not to be obstructed by a few facts and it would indeed be cavalier to wonder quite how the youthful protegés of the state school system provide any comparison with the largely business audience, often exclusively devoting their studies to French, catered for by Berlitz. Nevertheless, the market does seem to leave some remarkable gaps irrespective of the presumed sensitivity of its signalling mechanisms. The introduction by Unilever of New System Persil Automatic left Britain's 5 million eczema sufferers temporarily without a nationally available brand of automatic washing powder free of enzymes and other low temperature additives which are believed to cause irritation (*Guardian*, 7 April 1984).

Harbingers of doom: The Institute of Economic Affairs

Friends of the IEA and Social Affairs Unit featured prominently among the life peerages announced just before Christmas. (*Economic Affairs*, January 1983)

The role of the Institute of Economic Affairs has been of major importance in propagating pro-market critiques in Britain. What is most notable is the way in which the Institute has moved from the fringes of intellectual life to the centre, at least in terms of its relationship to mainstream policy developments. Ralph Harris, ennobled by Mrs Thatcher almost immediately after her 1979 victory, noted that

five years ago in Britain the radical critique of postwar thinking deployed by the Institute of Economic Affairs was still regarded as not quite cricket . . . As the rules for cricket were once handed down on tablets by the MCC, the rules for economic policy were set by the KCC: the Keynesian-Collectivist Consensus. (Harris, 1980)

The 1979 election however meant that 'the counter-revolution of market and monetary theory put the KCC team on the defensive' (*ibid.*, p. 11).

Central to the IEA case is the marked superiority of the economic market over the political market. In the former the picture is

. . . of consumers voting every day with their pennies and

pounds and choosing between the widest range of goods and services offered by competing producers, each with a powerful interest to cater for changing individual preferences. The structure of relative prices that spontaneously emerges serves as an information network that is not available in any other economic order ... In sharpest possible contrast stands the political market. It offers the citizen in a so-called democracy one vote every three or four years between two or three parties, each offering a massive package of policies and promises without any indication of their cost ... Where the economic market serves minorities on the basis of proportional representation, the winning party or coalition in the political market enforces all its policies on everyone – overriding minority and often majority preferences. Where market democracy rests on case-by-case consent for every item of consumption, political democracy relies inevitably on coercion ... In short, the market offers a wide choice of menus, all *à la carte*, with prices shown against each dish while government offers one gigantic 'free' lunch, on a *table d'hôte* take-it-or-leave-it basis with the undisclosed cost forcibly extracted from reluctant pockets through taxation. (*ibid.*, p. 15)

Harris argues that government is generally ill-equipped to deliver goods and services, that taxes constitute an ever-increasing burden on the private economy, with a marked disincentive effect, and that the problems of the poor are best dealt with through redistribution:

But what about those with insufficient financial 'votes' to acquire the necessaries for civilized living? The economic liberal's answer is that the poor are no more short of education, medical care or housing than they are of food, clothing or warmth. Their lack is not in frozen kind but in fluid cash. Their salvation is not through universal government provision of tax-financed services, but by selective redistribution which tops up low incomes to an acceptable minimum standard. In this way, the poor are enfranchized to vote in the market for essential goods and services that government does not have to provide. (*ibid.*, p. 23)

Harris, and others who have written under the auspices of the

Institute, have argued that the increasing involvement of government in managing the economy, providing social services and in direct industrial investment and production creates growing problems. Politicians are simply incapable of meeting the challenge:

> Even the best are unequal to the task of spending half the national income and supervising how much of the other half is deployed. They are unable to bring under control the once obedient servant of government that has grown since the war like a malignant Topsy. (Harris, p. 29)

As the economic crisis in Britain accelerated in the 1970s the Institute's voice became more strident. In 1975 Harris argued that, had advice for a radical rethinking on economic strategy been adopted in the 1960s, 'we should not now be facing an economic collapse that has led historians and political observers to see a breakdown in democratic institutions as itself politically possible' (Harris, 1975, p. 85).

The salvation of democracy

By the 1970s, claims that as a consequence of the dramatic expansion of the public sector western society was becoming increasingly ungovernable were commonplace. Monetarist and free-market critics argued that this was a consequence of a misconception of the proper role of government in the management of the economy and the provision of goods and services, and a failure to recognize the infinite superiority of market mechanisms in the delivery of most goods and services. They also drew attention to the political pressures which intensified the growth of the public sector, not least what they saw as the capacity of politicians continually to increase the stakes:

> The political arena is a marketplace in votes. Rival teams organize themselves to win a majority . . . The teams naturally and inevitably seek to outbid each other . . . There is no mechanism that requires the bid to be internally consistent or forces voters to balance more of one good against more of another. (Jay, 1977, p. 169)

The commitment to full employment was seen as having particularly pernicious consequences. Employers who met unreasonable wage demands subsequently experienced difficulty in making sales; in consequence unemployment increased. At this stage, however, governments intervened to restore full employment but the effect of this could only be inflationary. Peter Jay, son-in-law of the Labour Prime Minister, James Callaghan, and subsequently appointed by his government as ambassador in Washington, foresaw particularly disastrous consequences:

> So we reach the depressing conclusion that the operation of free democracy appears to force government into positions (the commitment to full employment) that prevent them from taking steps (fiscal and monetary restraint) that are necessary to arrest the menace (accelerating inflation) that threatens to undermine the condition (stable prosperity) on which political stability and therefore liberal democracy depend. In other words, democracy has itself by the tail and is eating itself up fast. (*ibid.*, p. 181)

Samuel Brittan, brother of the Conservative politician, and leading financial journalist, shared the concern over the apparently inexorable increase in the public's expectations of government:

> The generation of excessive expectations follows from the competitive nature of democracy . . . In their own private life, people know that more of one thing means less of something else on a given income and capital. In the absence of such knowledge in the political sphere, electorates tend to expect too much from government actions at too little cost . . . The temptation to encourage false expectations among the electorate thus becomes overwhelming to politicians. (Brittan, 1977, pp. 129-30)

Even the Duke of Edinburgh was moved to join in the general clamour of concern. In a broadcast on Radio Clyde, reprinted in an IEA collection of essays, the Duke offered the gloomy vision of increasing restrictions on the individual and an ever-more-powerful state:

> It looks as if we can expect to see an increasing bureaucratic involvement in virtually every aspect of the lives of individual

citizens . . . This will mean a gradual reduction in the freedom of choice in individual responsibility, particularly in such things as housing, the education of children, health care, the ability to acquire or inherit personal property, to hand on commercial enterprises, and the ability to provide for old age through personal savings and, perhaps most important of all, the freedom of the individual to exploit his skills or talents as suit him best. (Duke of Edinburgh, 1978, pp. 216-17)

In fact, for those not blessed with royal connections, many of the freedoms which the Duke regarded as of such central importance must have appeared somewhat marginal. Around 95 per cent of the population already relied on the state for their education and that of their children, few had private health care and even fewer commercial enterprises to hand on, while it is unclear how HRH related his own role to 'the freedom of the individual to exploit his skills or talents'.

It is worth emphasizing the stridency with which this view was being propagated, for it provides an important part of the backdrop to the election of the Thatcher government which was held by some to be the last real hope for reversing the drift. Patrick Cosgrave, a prominent Conservative journalist, regretting the failure of Edward Heath to reverse the trend, irrespective of his early efforts, argued:

It will require, in order to implement the Conservative doctrine that alone can prevent Britain from becoming wholly collectivized, both a far greater understanding of policy and a far deeper philosophical commitment than Mr Heath had in 1970 . . . But it is worth making the effort, since there hardly seems much point in political activity designed, as the Conservative defeatists suggested, merely to gain office at the head of a socialist state. What Churchill once called the long, drawling tides of defeat and surrender have been gaining force in the Conservative Party for a generation; it is with them that the Party has failed to cope, and the next chance may well be its last. (Cosgrave, 1977, p. 125)

The increasing amount of money spent by government on welfare services was a particular target for criticism. Such services were not only necessarily inefficient in organization and inflexible and unresponsive in delivery but served to preclude the development of alternatives by preempting the money available and the market demand for alternatives. This view is summarized by Arthur Seldon, with Harris the key figure in the IEA:

> Welfare as it *would* have developed without the welfare state would have been very different from welfare as it *was* in 1870, 1919 or 1946 before the welfare state. The question is whether by now voluntary welfare institutions would have been better or worse . . . I here argue that they would by now have far outshone the standardized, unresponsive, conservative, costly, politically distorted institutions of the welfare state. (Seldon, 1981, p. 16)

Indeed, Seldon argues that market pressures are in any case undermining state welfare as a consequence of consumer preference.

Journalist Paul Johnson who moved from the editorship of the *New Statesman* to the rather more rewarding pastures of the *Sunday Telegraph*, *The Times* and the *Daily Mail*, and to the far right of the political spectrum, suggested that the welfare state was responsible not only for economic decline but also for precipitating political violence:

> As the welfare state expands its activities, and increases its cost, so the wealth-creating sector contracts. But the state sector does not contract accordingly: it defends itself by inciting envy, and as envy remains unsatisfied – must, indeed, become even more dissatisfied as wealth-production falters and falls – so the urge to seek violent solutions, fostered by the moralistic propaganda of the welfare bureaucracy, increases. (Johnson, 1980, p. 9)

Johnson characteristically makes no attempt to demonstrate the accuracy of this monetarist nostrum, but it is worth noting that Britain's low growth rates went hand in hand with a level of social expenditure lower than that of many other countries with higher growth rates. OECD figures for 1981 show that social expenditure in the UK was 24.9 per cent of gross domestic product as against 31.5 per cent in Germany, whose postwar economic performance has far outstripped that of the UK. It is also worth noting that the United States with a significantly less developed welfare state remains a far more violent society than other western countries, a level of violence not confined simply to conventional crime but also spilling over into the political arena. It is equally notable that crime, particularly violent crime, increased under the Thatcher governments, while the NUM strike of 1984 and the massive police response saw political violence reach record postwar levels. In short, Johnson's attempt to link violence to the size of the welfare bureaucracy or pro-welfare views is at best disingenuous.

Monetarists, of course, no less than disciples of other theories of salvation, are inclined to exaggerate evidence which appears to substantiate their view, to ignore evidence which challenges it and to make some rather unusual interpretations of comparative data. Hence in his attack on the welfare state Seldon raises a favourite monetarist chestnut, the perceived effect of taxation in creating tax 'avoision' which he defines as 'an amalgam of avoidance and evasion' (Seldon, 1981, p. 14). High taxation is of course one of the objectionable consequences of state welfare. Seldon suggests that tax evasion, which in contrast to tax avoidance is illegal, might account for 25 per cent of earnings: 'Tax evasion, officially estimated at 7½ per cent of earnings, unofficially (by Professor Edgar Feige) at 15 per cent or more, but conceivably nearer 25 per cent, is a measure of rejection of the welfare state in particular as well as of intrusive over-government in general' (*ibid.*, p. 14). Since most PAYE recipients have minimal opportunities to evade tax this suggests that others are evading tax at a truly spectacular rate.

Harris has been equally cavalier in throwing out figures for the alleged economic damage caused by high tax rates. He quotes approvingly Arthur Laffer's proposition that beyond a certain point increasing tax rates produce a diminishing revenue since the disincentive will result in a decline in economic output and in consequence in total tax revenue: 'A recent, admittedly crude, econometric assessment of the effects of the British tax burden led Dr Michael Beenstock to surmise that "the marginal cost of £1 of revenue in terms of disincentive effects is approximately £3"' (Harris, 1980, p. 17). The pursuit of such 'supply side' economics and the consequent tax cuts for the rich in the United States resulted in spectacular increases in the American budget deficit and growing social inequality.

It is in any case particularly difficult to argue that on the one hand tax 'avoision' has reached epidemic proportions and that on the other taxation exercises a strong disincentive effect. Lekachman, a leading American economist, in a withering attack on the American proponents of monetarism and supply-side economics asks, not unreasonably, why the explosion of activity promised by the advocates of tax cuts has not already taken place:

> Broadly speaking, taxes on capital gains, large incomes, and corporate profits have been steadily declining for a dozen years. For practical purposes, Congress has been quietly phasing out the corporate profits tax as a revenue source. Any corporate executive worthy of his spurs negotiates the sort of contract with his employer that confers substantial sums upon him completely sheltered from tax. Why, it might legitimately be asked, haven't these amply rewarded managers and investors already unleashed the investment boom needed to renew economic growth and make America great again? (Lekachman, 1982, p. 62)

We will return to some other problems in supply-side economics after a brief glance at another instance of facts meaning not what they mean but whatever you want them to mean.

In an attack on the National Health Service published by the pro-free enterprise, Aims of Industry, Ralph Howell, Conservative MP, who we are told 'has specialized knowledge of agriculture, social affairs, taxation and the welfare system', claims that the health service is vastly overstaffed. In support of this argument Howell cites the fact that the number of staff per bed occupied has increased dramatically since 1960 when 'a total staff of 565,000 cared for 478,000 bed patients', in contrast to now when with staff at an all-time high of 1,287,000 only 365,000 beds are occupied (Howell, 1983, p. 4). As further evidence of overstaffing he specifically cites the increase in the number of doctors and nurses. Yet turning to Seldon's defence of the relative merits of the American health-care system over the British, we find the suggestion that one demonstration of the superiority of the American system is to be found in the fact that 'there are now probably twice as many doctors, dentists, midwives and nurses per hospital patient in the USA as in the UK' (Seldon, 1981,

p. 24). For Seldon this demonstrates not overstaffing but the greater market sensitivity of the American system. We will have cause to examine in more detail some of the wilder arguments and claims made about the health service in a subsequent chapter.

Enter the supply-siders

> What the poor need most of all in order to succeed is the spur of their poverty. (George Gilder, *Wealth and Poverty*, 1982)

The doubtful benefits of supply-side economics have been more widely advertised and advocated in the United States. They were popularly articulated by an American Congressman Jack Kemp, a former professional footballer with the Buffalo Bills and a possible candidate for the Presidency in 1988. It is undoubtedly this exposure to the roughest and toughest of American competition which has given Kemp a unique insight into the operation of the marketplace; indeed Kemp quotes for approval an exchange with a correspondent from the magazine *Politics Today*:

> PT: In several interviews you've given great credit to the economists and so on, and you don't pretend, you say, to be an expert in economics: although that's now arguable, I take it.

> Kemp: Well, right about now I would say I am an expert in incentive . . . I played quarterback for about 27 of my 35 years in organized and professional football. I was president of the Football Players' Union. I bargained collectively on behalf of the players. I operated in an environment which was basically very marginal, to the extent that everything you do in professional football as quarterback is on the margin. You're in the huddle, you get 30 seconds, you call the play. Either it works or it doesn't. Your success is easily measurable. You have three seconds to get the ball, get back, and choose a receiver from four or five different possibilities. It's incentive. It's price theories. A reward-risk ratio (Kemp, 1980, pp. 32 and 33)

Indeed, football metaphors litter Kemp's work, though given that the UK has a Prime Minister who believes the economics of managing a household are the key to successful management of the economy, it is well not to be too scathing. In contrast to the more rigorous denunciation of state provision put forward by groups such as the IEA, Kemp is prepared to allow some role for the public sector in the context, of course, of the massive unleashing of economic prosperity generated by supply-side policies:

> A prosperous private economy can easily afford a strong safety net of public services. A stifled smothering economy can't. A prosperous economy can afford to care for our elderly, police our neighbourhoods, school our children, and pave our roads. Private affluence does not mean public squalor. (*ibid.*, p. 96)

In practice, however, it is difficult to see any significant role for welfarist measures in supply-side policies.

The key to understanding supply-side economics lies in its focus on the desirability of tax cuts as a means of unleashing prodigious new energies in the economy. These, together with the abolition of unnecessary government regulations, such as for example attempts to control the utilization of energy and other conservation measures, will produce dramatic growth.

> Does anyone doubt that the American people would respond to the incentives that such reasonable tax rates will provide? Does anyone doubt that there will be an explosion of real economic activity? . . . *We are now operating at less than half our potential, perhaps less than a third our potential!* There's no telling what we can accomplish if only the government would get out of the way and let us load the wagon. (*ibid.*, pp. 10 and 11; emphasis in original)

In common with monetarists and free marketeers, Kemp, notwithstanding his opposition to 'public squalor', is eager to attribute social problems to government intervention. He argues that youth unemployment is a consequence of minimum wage legislation which has priced teenagers out of work. As the minimum wage level rose so did the level of youth unemployment: 'The minimum wage law became a total barrier to opportunity, in effect a 100 per cent tax rate on black teenagers!' (*ibid.*, p. 42). This conveniently avoids any discussion of possible changes in the labour market which may have reduced the demand for certain kinds of labour. Kemp, like Friedman, finds comfort in the proposition that in a free market wages would find their own level and full employment would be achieved. Kemp argues that government intervention destroys creativity:

> A thousand people can grow up to produce opera, Broadway musicals or a *Wizard of Oz*. A few generations later with government in the way, a thousand people are born to create; but of the fraction of these who survive the system, many end up making porno. Instead of several thousand restaurants worthy of three stars in the *New York Times*, we get 10,000 plastic restaurants (*ibid.*, pp. 7 and 8)

Quite what public subsidy of the opera has to do with the first or health regulations with the latter is unclear. Certainly if any credit is to be taken for the growth of the porno industry it should be firmly placed where it belongs – in the role of the market.

Whatever the limitations on Kemp's grasp of economics, he was successful in having elements of his proposals adopted by the Reagan administration. The Kemp-Roth tax cut, introduced in August 1981, was intended to precipitate the boom in the American economy that the supply-siders had promised. In practice the primary beneficiaries were upper-income tax payers. Lekachman argued:

> Approximately 85 per cent of the benefits will accrue to tax payers above annual incomes of $50,000. This is supply-side economics with a vengeance, a wager on the behaviour of the already affluent. If the rich do their job, a new investment boom and a new surge of entrepreneurial innovation will vastly accelerate growth and allow its benefits to trickle down from the intrepid, gifted minority to humbler Americans, less individually and financially gifted. (Lekachman, 1982, p. 67)

In the United States a programme of tax cuts was introduced hand in hand with increasing stringency in the administration of benefits to the unemployed and other low-income groups, leaving Galbraith to argue that the left owed a considerable debt to Ronald Reagan for exposing with particular clarity the administration's bias towards the rich:

> More to be acknowledged is President Reagan's far-from-insignificant service on the matter of supply-side economics. The basic case here was that the rich were not working and

investing because they were receiving too little money and that the poor were not working because they were getting too much. The magic word was incentive – incentives for both the rich and the poor. (Galbraith, 1983, p. 15)

In fact, the Reagan administration adopted not only supply-side strategies but also monetarist strategies irrespective of the fact that, as Lekachman has argued, they point in contradictory directions:

Supply-side policies clash directly with monetarism, the success of the former requires easy credit, low interest rates, and a resulting boom in investment. Monetarism can slaughter the inflation dragon only by starving the economy of funds for new machines and factories, and keeping interest rates high enough for long enough to shove the economy into a good, old-fashioned recession (Lekachman, 1982, p. 17)

Subsequently the Reagan administration dropped all pretence of maintaining monetarist targets and proceeded to fuel the American recovery by committing a cardinal monetarist sin, the creation of a dramatically larger budget deficit.

The particularly uplifting contribution which supply-side economics could make to the moral character of the poor was dwelt on at more length by another supply-side popularizer, George Gilder.

In a series of books, Gilder has drawn attention to the allegedly debilitating effects of welfare on the structure of the family, sex roles and the work incentive made by welfare payments. Gilder believes quite unashamedly in the merit of incentives via tax cuts for the rich and benefit cuts for the poor: ' . . . an effort to take income from the rich, thus diminishing their investment, and to give it to the poor, thus reducing their work incentives, is sure to cut American productivity, limit job opportunities, and perpetuate poverty' (Gilder, 1982, p. 73). Gilder is exercised by what he sees as the corrosive effect of welfare on the family structure, particularly that of low-income black Americans. He argues that

welfare still erodes the sexual constitution of society . . . The sexual constitution of welfare is particularly disastrous for young men. It tells them money is a bequest for women rather than the earnings of men. It indirectly deprives them of the example of a male provider in the home. In conjunction with the absence of jobs and apprenticeships for youth, it discourages the early acquisition of work habits and employment records. (Gilder, 1974, pp. 166-7)

Gilder's argument hangs on two linked propositions, firstly that welfare undermines work incentives, and secondly that the major role in the labour market should properly be taken by men and that the consequence of welfare is simultaneously to undermine work incentives and to attack the male role as provider:

Most American men earn more money than their wives; men that don't tend to leave, or be left, in large numbers. Yet poor men are assumed to be unaffected by the high relative incomes available to their wives from welfare and affirmative action, which are alleged to have no relationship to high rates of unemployment and illegitimacy (Gilder, 1982, p. 71)

In an earlier book, *The Visible Man*, Gilder had sought to trace and interpret the career of a young black, Mitchell Brewer, held on a rape charge. With a blissful lack of concern for the problems posed in any attempt to understand and reconstruct a series of events through the interpretations of participants' and observers' descriptions, not to mention the reductionist absurdity of attempting to draw general conclusions from one case, Gilder found the answer to his quest in the welfare culture and its alleged effects on attitudes to work and the proliferation of fatherless families. Indeed, liberals had not only conspired to place the young black in an intolerable welfare culture but now, in their insistence on legal reforms which would protect the alleged victims of rape cases from questions regarding their sexual behaviour, they would prohibit a line of defence which ultimately secured Mitchell Brewer's acquittal (Gilder, 1978, pp. 185-6). These themes – the welfare trap created by well-intentioned but misconceived liberal attitudes to social reform, the responsibility of young blacks for 'the bad "conditions" they largely create' (*ibid.*, p. xi), and the deleterious cultural effects of women stepping into roles which should properly be reserved for men – are central to Gilder's political stance.

Gilder's argument is not restricted to the reassertion of 'women's proper place' and attacks on lavish welfare, it is also based, in common with other supply-side arguments, on an assertion of the need for greater social inequality. It is only by allowing the very rich to become even richer that ordinary mortals will have any hope of achieving even a modest prosperity: 'Entrepreneurs must be allowed to retain wealth for the practical reason that only they, collectively, can possibly know where it should go, to whom it should be given' (Gilder, 1982, p. 27). This proposition is based on the belief that market mechanisms are the only ones which guarantee an effective allocation of resources, but that in order to take advantage of them the rich must be allowed to retain most of the gains made both to provide incentives for investment and cash for future investment. In contrast to the monetarists, however, but perhaps consistent with his antediluvian ontological assumptions, Gilder reserves the role of *dramatis personae* to the rugged individualist:

> It is these capitalists, extending the division of labour by launching new goods and services, who expand the market, not the other way around. It is these often self-denying explorers beyond the bounds of the existing marketplace and its prevailing goods and services who extend the frontiers of human possibility, not some impersonal mechanism of exchange. (*ibid.*, pp. 32-3)

These entertaining if arcane nostrums would be of less concern were it not for the fact that David Stockman, then Director of the Office of Management and the Budget in the Reagan administration, described Gilder's book, *Wealth and Poverty*, as 'Promethean in its intellectual power and insight' and were it not apparently held to have some almost biblical qualities for Ronald Reagan, who even held it up on national TV (Lekachman, 1982, p. 51).

It is perhaps worth noting that in the introduction to the British edition of this book, in a no doubt understandable fit of enthusiasm, Gilder manages to elect the Thatcher government in 1978 (*op. cit.*, p. xvii) and suggests that the 'utterly stifling' tax rates inherited by the Thatcher government were 'an incredible 60 per cent on earnings of £12,501, reaching 83 per cent at just £24,000 and 98 per cent on unearned incomes.' These were indeed draconian levels of taxation, but it is unclear which groups were actually experiencing them. According to calculations reported in the *Guardian* in 1978-9 the percentage of income taken at £10,000 averaged 23.2 per cent, at £20,000 29.8 per cent, at £30,000 39.4 per cent, and at £40,000 47.7 per cent (17 March 1983).

Perhaps like the monetarists the supply-siders sometimes find that their enthusiasm for salvation renders their grasp on the present tenuous. Certainly the level of taxes described by Gilder would indeed be stifling and perhaps, as he argued, 'Further substantial cuts in personal income tax rates, particularly in the top bracket and on investment income, could foster an exciting revival of enterprise in Britain without any cost in government revenues' (*ibid.*, p. xxi). However, if the tax rates were in reality less than half those claimed by Gilder, one is inclined to wonder why the explosion of economic activity was not already taking place. In any case, as we will see, in spite of significant tax cuts for the very rich under the Thatcher government, not only was there no revival of enterprise, exciting or otherwise, but the cost in government revenue was in part met by tax increases on middle- and lower-income groups. If the supply-siders are wrong about the economic boom consequent upon tax handouts to the rich, there will also be no compensating increase in government revenue consequent upon the growth of GNP which such a revival would have created. In the UK, given the government's unwillingness to increase the size of the public sector borrowing requirement, tax cuts for the rich inevitably left the poor paying more.

In the United States, where the support for supply-side economics was both stronger and more explicit, the consequence of tax cuts to the rich was, as might have been expected, to increase the affluence of their lifestyles. There was not however any consequent economic revival, and the economic revival when it did occur seemed to have more to do with the escalating size of the public sector deficit. The benefits of supply-side economics to the bulk of the population remain unclear, as Lekachman put it: 'A large segment of the population is still waiting for its invitation to the party. The poverty population . . . has increased by 30 per cent since 1981' (*New Society*, 1984, p. 176). One study found that amongst the poorest one-fifth of families in the United States disposable income fell by 9.4 per cent between 1979 and 1984 (*Dissent*, Spring 1984, p. 174).

The supply-siders also share with the monetarists an opposition to what are seen as excessive welfare programmes and to other government programmes directed to equality of opportunity.

> Welfare now erodes work and family and thus keeps poor people poor. Accompanying welfare is an ideology – sustaining a whole system of federal and state bureaucracies – that also operates to destroy their faith. The ideology takes the form of false theories of discrimination and spurious claims of racism and sexism as the dominant forces in the lives of the poor. The bureaucracies are devoted to 'equal opportunity' and 'affirmative action'. Together they compete with welfare in their pernicious influence on the poor – most especially the poor who happen to be black. (Gilder, 1982, p. 128)

In any case, of course, for Gilder such intervention is misconceived in the case of women since it has a deleterious effect on 'formerly settled roles' (*ibid.*, p. 15) and in the case of blacks it is unnecessary since racism is not a significant factor in the US labour market: 'Liberals are not racists any more than all but a small, dwindling, and utterly uninfluential minority of other Americans are' (*ibid.*, p. 71).

Organizations set up to tackle supposed discrimination are alleged to have an inherent self-interest in magnifying its supposed extent, a point made by new-right philosopher Anthony Flew in reference to the British Commission for Racial Equality, whose approach he describes as being based on a 'neo-Marxist conception of racism'. Flew argues:

> It is perhaps just worth remarking, by the way, that the Commission itself is a quango. All its members, therefore, as well as its many employees, both direct and indirect, whether they realize it or not, have obvious job-protection interest in making the most of the extent of the evil which they are commissioned to encounter. (Flew, 1984, pp. 3 and 4)

In general, government intervention is regarded as misconceived, frequently motivated by an anti-business ethic, and disruptive of the efficient operation of market mechanisms. Hence groups like the Environmental Protection Agency and the Food and Drug Administration are opposed by Gilder as blocking business innovation and economic growth: 'Throughout the world, people live longest in the most industrialized, dynamic, and polluted countries – and longevity continues to rise in industrial societies – the burden of proof should normally fall on those who wish to halt progress in the name of saving lives (Gilder, 1982, p. 232). Monetarists do not all share Gilder's cavalier approach to environmental issues, but they too are unsympathetic to direct government regulation, preferring pricing mechanisms, for example, on effluent discharge as a more attractive alternative. Some are quite explicitly prepared to sacrifice some environmental quality in return for economic growth (Beckerman, 1975).

The return to the family

Supply-siders and monetarists are also united in their common emphasis on the importance of the family. For Margaret Thatcher the family is an integral part of the competitive individualism she advocates:

> The sense of being self-reliant, of playing a role within the family, of owning one's own property, of paying one's way, are all part of the spiritual ballast which maintains responsible citizenship, and provides a solid foundation from which people look around to see what more they might do for others and for themselves. (Thatcher, 1977, p. 97)

Sir Keith Joseph has also set the family in a wider economic context: 'The family must be the centre of our thinking . . . a large part of our production and services comes from the family firms which are the backbone of economic and community life . . . The indispensable basis not just of economic vitality but also of political liberties' (Fitzgerald, 1983, p. 55).

Patrick Minford, a leading British monetarist who has argued for the complete dismantling of the welfare state, has made the responsibility of the family explicit:

> The provision of direct social services is regarded by many as something that the family should undertake. When the state provides these services, there is serious concern that families feel morally justified in abandoning their responsibilities to the state. This is an unhappy situation . . . Society rightly feels that elderly parents and relatives, for example . . . are the

responsibility of next of kin to help. The same is true of handicapped children. (Minford, 1984)

Patrick Minford recognizes that not all families will share this
view but the solution is straightforward:

The logical action to take is therefore for such responsibilities
to be made legally mandatory, just as child battering or child
neglect are penalized by the law. Neglect of these family
responsibilities would be actionable by the state ... Social
services will be necessary, just as police are necessary to
maintain law and order. (*ibid.*)

For supply-siders like Gilder, the family is the crucial arena in
which the male breadwinner comes into his own: 'The only
dependable route from poverty is always work, family and faith'
(Gilder, 1982, p. 74). In contrast:

... to a great extent poverty and unemployment, and even the
largely psychological conditions of 'unemployability' are
chiefly reflections of family deterioration ... Nothing is so
destructive to all these male values as the growing, imperious
recognition that when all is said and done his wife and children
can do better without him. The man has the gradually sinking
feeling that his role of provider, the definitive male activity
from the primal days of the hunt through the industrial revolution and on into modern life, has been largely seized from
him; he has been cuckolded by the compassionate state.
(*ibid.*, p. 118)

In the light of calls for a major reduction in state involvement
in social welfare and in the economy, emphasis on the family not
only offers a context within which the individual seeks a wider
self-realization and meaning, but also provides an alternative
source of support and welfare. Indeed, as we will see, this emphasis on the family and the wider community provides a central
plank in new-right thinking about social welfare. Here as elsewhere, however, we are not simply dealing with an opportunistic
response to the exigencies of public sector cutbacks, but to an
integral aspect of the new right's broader social and economic
philosophy. The family is the central social institution, while

society and the management of the economy are frequently seen in terms redolent of domestic life and family imagery.

The new authoritarians

> Even democracy can be discarded without detriment to the civic wellbeing as the Conservative conceives it. (Roger Scruton, 1980)

While the monetarist wing of the new right had emphasized the centrality of markets, there was also a tradition within Conservative philosophy firmly wedded to the centrality of private property, but more concerned with questions of tradition and authority than with particular economic theories. American new-right author, Irving Kristol, suggested that the very success and affluence of market societies created a particular kind of existential problem:

> One is led to question the validity of the original liberal idea that it is possible for the individual, alone or in purely voluntary association with others, to cope with the eternal dilemmas of the human condition. The moral authority of tradition, and some public support for this authority, seems to be needed. (Kristol, 1978)

Kristol, while not denying that the market has some proper role in the economy, argues that its outcomes cannot provide a satisfactory moral basis for social cohesion:

> My reading of history is that, in the same way that men cannot for long tolerate a sense of spiritual meaninglessness in their individual lives, so they cannot for long accept a society in which power, privilege and property are not distributed according to some morally meaningful criteria ... So I conclude, despite Professor Hayek's ingenious analysis, that men cannot accept the historical accidents of the marketplace – seen merely as accidents – as the basis for an enduring and legitimate entitlement to power, privilege and property. (Kristol, 1973, pp. 97-8)

What is needed then is some alternative form of legitimacy and authority: 'Though the discontents of our civilization express themselves in the "rhetoric of liberation" and "equality", one can detect beneath the surface an acute yearning for order and stability – but a legitimate order, of course, and a legitimized stability' (*ibid.*, p. 105).

In the UK too there were Conservatives on the right who were far from wedded to monetarist and free-market doctrines, nor did they find it necessary to dress up their argument as the defence of individualism and liberty. Roger Scruton, who achieved increasing prominence as a new-right publicist, argued in *The Meaning of Conservatism* against the concern with reform and change which appeared to dominate the Conservative Party:

> Most of all, it has begun to see itself as the defender of individual freedom against the encroachment of the state, concerned to return to the people their natural right of choice, and to inject into every corporate body the healing principle of democracy. These are passing fashions . . . but by no means the ineluctable expression of the Conservative point of view . . . Even democracy – which corresponds neither to the natural nor to the supernatural yearnings of the normal citizen – can be discarded without detriment to the civic wellbeing as the Conservative conceives it (Scruton, 1980, pp. 15 and 16)

In perhaps a prescient insight into the trend of the future, Scruton regretted that 'Politicians and especially politicians of the "moderate" right have lost their nerve' and failed to prosecute the left for subversion as the law of sedition, as he conceived it, demanded (*ibid.*, pp. 17 and 18). A use of state power which he thought could be particularly directed against militant trade unionists.

Scruton, like Kristol, was unsympathetic to the apostles of monetarism:

> A citizen's allegiance requires fixed expectations, a settled sense of his own and others' material status, and a sense that he is not the victim of uncontrollable forces that might at any moment plunge him into destitution or raise him to incomprehensible wealth . . . This argues not for a free market but for something like its opposite . . . Indeed, it has led to the acceptance by the Conservative Party of economic theories – such as that of Keynes – which regard the interference of the state in

the market process as a social and economic necessity. (*ibid.*)

Notwithstanding these reservations, Scruton became an enthusiastic acolyte of Thatcherism, urging the government on to new frontiers in the pages of *The Times*. Faced with the uproar created by the government's plans to abolish the Metropolitan Authorities and the Greater London Council, Scruton had no hesitation:

> Far better, to abolish elections altogether and to return to local government on the medieval model – by the Sovereign's command. If attendance at Council meetings were a duty, like jury service – imposed upon citizens of sufficient public standing for a limited period, and with no prospect of reward, then the result would be precisely what the Conservative Party is seeking. (*The Times*, 18 October 1983)

Through the *Salisbury Review* and the Conservative Philosophy Group, Scruton and other like-minded Conservatives, sometimes known as the Peterhouse School, continued to push forward an authoritarian, nationalistic vision of Conservatism. The CPG achieved some prominence as a debating circle, often meeting at the house of Jonathan Aitken MP and attracting such well-known figures as John Selwyn Gummer, Julian Amery, Enoch Powell and on occasion Margaret Thatcher. An article in *The Times* (31 January 1983) discussed the group under the heading: 'Who thinks for Mrs Thatcher?'

The alliance between monetarists proclaiming freedom through the market and anti-libertarian traditionalists may have been opportunist but it provided the means of appealing to two distinct constituencies. It also afforded intellectual support for the authoritarian direction in which the Thatcher government moved. The traditionalists offered uncritical backing to the suppression of those conflicts unleashed by market forces. In their public posturings the traditionalists concentrated on urging the government to ever more draconian measures, whether the repatriation of immigrants, advocated by Cambridge don John Casey in the first issue of the *Salisbury Review* (Autumn 1982), the further centralization of power or the restriction of trade unions (Scruton, 1984). In practice there was remarkably little public dispute between the two groups. Members of the Peterhouse School, like Scruton, may have supported the welfare state (Scruton, 1983) while the IEA enthusiastically urged its dismantling, but little of these conflicts surfaced in public debate.

One reason for this apparent accord between authoritarians and monetarists may be found in the fact that while authoritarians were, in principle, in favour of government intervention in the welfare area they joined with monetarists in opposing 'throwing money at social problems'. The solutions to problems of crime and deviance were commonly seen to lie in the area of law and order and both groups could unite on suggestions that soft welfare measures were responsible for accelerating social problems, not resolving them. In the words of A. Crawford, a commentator on the American scene, 'Just as liberals have been accused by Conservatives of throwing dollars at problems, the right would in effect, throw bombs' (Crawford, 1980, p. 89).

The ease with which the upholders of firm government and a revitalized moral order embraced those who claimed the market pre-eminent and capitalism triumphant as the road to salvation was nonetheless remarkable. In 1971 Tory literatus John Selwyn Gummer was commenting on the destructive effects of modern capitalism in a manner usually associated with those on the communitarian left of the spectrum:

> The whole tendency of modern capitalism is towards the destruction of such communities as do exist. We have seen the effects of the frenetic exploitation of the new which is so essential a part of the marketing strategy of mass production. New public housing and the tearing down of the slums paradoxically destroys rather than promotes community . . . the pressure put on our citizens to compete for material possessions has already destroyed the concept of the extended family and is now busy pulling the nuclear family of parents and young children apart as women rush out to work to earn enough to keep up with the Joneses. (Gummer, 1971, pp. 168-9)

In the course of a general attack on permissiveness, Gummer argued that the state 'has to accept that its decisions or lack of decisions on moral issues are going to have the most direct bearing upon the environment in which each new generation grows up and that fundamentally concerns the community' (*ibid.*, p. 65).

By 1984 Gummer had leapt to minor prominence as Chairman of the Conservative Party and member of a Cabinet which, while it no doubt met Mr Gummer's concern about the effects of public housing by largely ceasing to finance its construction, appeared to share none of his concerns about the deleterious effects of an unrestrained capitalism.

Conclusion

In office the Thatcher government was to draw on a range of ideologies in harnessing support. Monetarism was to be allied to jingoism and authoritarianism in pursuit of the new Conservative hegemony. Whilst free-market economists advocated the minimal state and the maximum degree of individual liberty, protected through the market, the government sought to centralize more and more power in its own hands and those of its acolytes. The apparently contradictory nature of some of the government's policy directions would not necessarily have been apparent to ministers who frequently seemed to display only the vaguest understanding of the economic theories with which they were directing the nation's destiny. Christopher Huhne, the Economics Editor of the *Guardian*, has succinctly illustrated this point by drawing attention to Mrs Thatcher's response to a TV interview with Peter Jay, in which she was asked whether she believed that Britain had yet reached the 'natural rate' of unemployment at which, according to monetarists, inflation would stop or at least cease to accelerate. The notion of a natural rate of unemployment, as Huhne argues, was crucial to the government's case against public spending, which it claimed would create inflation and not jobs. The Prime Minister's answer 'delivered in such a way under repeated questioning that no-one could be in any serious doubt of her ignorance' missed the point completely and moved into the entirely extraneous issue of the current account surplus:

> It's not a doctrine to which I have subscribed. It's one which I think actually came in with Milton Friedman. I used to read about it, I used to look about it (sic) and not adopt it. It's a theory to which I have never subscribed. At the moment in spite of 3¼ million unemployed, we have a current account

surplus – we have had a current account surplus for five years in a row. (Huhne, 1985)

The Prime Minister's forte was evidently in nurturing fears that Britain was being 'swamped' by immigrants, in appeals to patriotic unity in the face of the threat to our way of life in the South Atlantic and in the reduction of economics to a series of dictums drawn from life in the parlour behind the Grantham grocery store.

2. The Emergence of Snobby Roberts

She doesn't tell us she was known at school as 'snobby' Roberts; *she doesn't tell us everything.* (Arnold, 1984)

Which welfare backlash?

Some writers, notably those on the Marxist left, have argued that the election of the Thatcher government in 1979 represented a significant shift in popular attitudes to the welfare state. The success of the Conservatives in 1979 was, it has been suggested, in no small measure attributable to the way in which they had been able to capitalize on popular discontent. The ideology of the new right found a popular resonance in people's everyday experience:

> Thatcher's style was to translate the themes of the new economic liberalism into slogans and ideas that tapped popular discontent with many aspects of the present state, such as the arbitrariness of bureaucracy, the inefficiency of nationalized industry, the burden of taxation, the 'privileges' enjoyed by immigrants, the damage of strikes, the lawlessness of demonstrations and the undermining of the independence and moral responsibility of families. (Gamble, 1981, p. 150)

Thatcher, it is argued, was able to capitalize on widespread dissatisfaction with the modern state, not least with the way in which it delivered welfare services. She offered the discontented an alternative perspective to the traditional Butskellite consensus: she presented welfare not as something worth fighting for, or as a reflection of social altruism, but rather as an alien imposition financed by taxes wrung from working people, primarily for the benefit of an ever-growing army of bureaucrats and scroungers.

Peter Leonard, a leading Marxist expert on welfare, commented in the wake of the 1979 Conservative victory:

> This new historical moment reflects the successful ideological offensive by the radical right in securing the ground lost by social democratic politics and ideology. The working class has been deeply penetrated by this offensive, not least in the field of welfare where its experience of oppressive and alien welfare structures has appeared to authenticate right-wing ideas. (Leonard, 1979, p. 13)

Trade union leader Bernard Dix talked of the 'acceptance of a new configuration of popular and authoritarian rightism' and argued that 'Thatcher was able to convince large numbers of voters that the problems of that period (the 1970s) were due to an excess of state interference in economic affairs'. Paul Corrigan, another Marxist academic, wrote of a 'distinct vote against the welfare state' and 'a real shift away from social democracy to the right', a shift based in part on the negative experience of welfare programmes which failed to deliver their promise: 'Comprehensives have not ended selection since that selection occurs within the examination system; the NHS has not provided an open experience of a good health service; council housing is not widely experienced as a democratic housing form etc.' (Corrigan, 1979, p. 15)

Such arguments were widely accepted and caused a considerable amount of strategic rethinking on the left, but though they contained within them some important acknowledgements of the limitations of the postwar welfare state they also credited Thatcherism with considerably more popular coherence and support than seems merited. Indeed there is no evidence to suggest that 1979 or even the preceding period marks some decisive turning point in public opinion about welfare. In Thatcher's election to the leadership of the Conservative Party and in the subsequent electoral campaign the future of the welfare state was simply not a major public topic. To the extent that it surfaced as an issue the Conservative response was to try to allay any suggestion that they intended to dismantle the welfare state. Welfare would be more efficient, bureaucratic fat would be removed and scroungers penalized but there was no wider attack on the principle of state welfare provision. It is true that important elements in the

Conservative Party, including Margaret Thatcher, were profoundly unsympathetic to state welfare provision. But it is a quantum leap to move from this to the assertion that the election of the Thatcher government reflected either a widespread acknowledgement of this position or, even more, a growing level of public support for it. There was always a strong constituency within the Conservative Party, and indeed in the wider electorate, who were unsympathetic to redistributive social programmes and whose solution to social problems was punitive rather than reformative. Delinquents were to be flogged not rehabilitated. The solution to inner-city riots may lie in public spending, but it would be on water cannon rather than public housing.

Firstly, it should be clear that the Conservative victory in 1979 was not by any stretch of the imagination of decisive historical proportions. With 43.9 per cent of the votes cast, Margaret Thatcher came to power with the smallest proportion received by any majority party since 1922.

Attitudes to welfare spending, as reflected in opinion surveys, vary over time but there is no evidence of mounting opposition to the social services of the kind identified, for example, by Corrigan. A 1980 MORI survey found considerable support for cuts in social security benefits: 44 per cent favoured a cut as against 9 per cent who favoured an increase. However, only 5 per cent favoured a cut in spending on education as against 36 per cent who favoured an increase, 5 per cent favoured a cut in NHS spending as against a massive 57 per cent who favoured an increase. Even in the area of local authority housing the number favouring an increase, 28 per cent, was twice the number favouring a cut, 14 per cent (Lansley and Weir, 1983, p. 284).

Far from Thatcher having placed herself at the head of an increasing army of individualists eager to dismantle the welfare state, subsequent opinion polls were to show a marked increase in support for welfare. By 1983 the number favouring a cut in spending on education had fallen to 3 per cent and those favouring an increase had risen to 55 per cent; only 2 per cent favoured a cut in NHS spending, 59 per cent favoured an increase. On social security benefits the number favouring a cut had fallen from 44 to 23 per cent and those favouring an increase had risen from 9 to 19 per cent (*ibid.*). A 1976 EEC survey had found that 43 per cent of the British blamed the poor for their own poverty, attributing it to 'laxness and lack of willpower', in contrast to 10 per cent who blamed it on 'injustice'. By 1983 only 23 per cent blamed the poor and 33 per cent blamed injustice (*ibid.*). These shifts in opinion were no doubt accelerated by the dramatic increases in unemployment engendered by the economic policies of the Thatcher government, nonetheless they caution against the ready acceptance of the view that the Thatcher victory was in any way significantly associated with a welfare backlash. Equally, the subsequent Conservative victory in 1983 appears to have been largely unaffected by the apparent change in sentiment towards support for a more generous provision of social services.

A survey conducted prior to the 1983 election found little support for the government's spending priorities. When respondents were asked which items of government spending would be their highest priority for additional spending 37 per cent ranked health and 24 per cent ranked education first. In contrast defence was ranked first by only 4 per cent, and police and prisons, the other major beneficiaries of increased public spending under the Thatcher government, by only 3 per cent. When respondents were asked whether they favoured keeping taxes and spending on social services at the same level, reducing taxes and spending less, or increasing taxes and spending more, 54 per cent favoured the status quo. More significantly, whereas 32 per cent favoured an increase in taxes to allow for greater spending only 9 per cent favoured reducing taxes. The government's belief in the economic and social damage inflicted by welfare obviously was not widely shared. The government's concern to price the unemployed back into work was also supported by only a minority. Forty-six per cent of respondents thought that unemployment benefits were too low and caused hardship as against only 35 per cent who believed that they were too high and discouraged people from finding jobs (Bosanquet, 1984).

The view that there was a growing backlash against welfare was not peculiar to the Marxist left; it was also one which was carefully cultivated by the Institute of Economic Affairs (see Harris and Seldon, 1979). In a series of opinion surveys the Institute reported an increasing amount of support for the market provision of services 'for a radical change that will permit individuals freedom to contract out of state education and health services' (*ibid.*, p. 59). The IEA evidence is, however, unreliable, depending on a somewhat unusual treatment of the data and what some critics described as 'a determination to rectify opinions in line with anticipated conclusions' (Judge, Smith and Taylor-Gooby, 1983, p. 5; see also Taylor-Gooby, 1982).

A more accurate reading of the 1979 Conservative electoral victory would place the emphasis elsewhere. The Labour government's apparent failure to manage the economy and more particularly the 'winter of discontent' undoubtedly affected the outcome. More important than Thatcher's hostility to the welfare state was her widely publicized promise, in 1979, to cut taxation. As Kellner has shown, increased taxation had fallen particularly heavily on average and lower-paid workers: 'In 1951 the manager paid the same amount in tax and national insurance as five male manual workers. Today, those five manual workers are, between them, paying almost twice as much as an equivalent manager' (Kellner, 1981). Some former Labour voters, particularly amongst skilled workers, were no doubt seduced by the chimera of tax cuts but attitudes towards welfare cannot simply be deduced from attitudes towards taxation. Tax cuts at least in theory might simply have been financed by the promised attack on waste and inefficiency.

For those who saw a widespread international turn to the right it is perhaps also worth noting that the evidence from the United States suggests that the election of Ronald Reagan in 1980 reflected neither the victory of the 'moral majority' nor any sudden conversion of the American electorate to new-right policies. A survey by Mueller, focusing on the conservative opposition to feminist issues such as abortion and the Equal Rights Amendment, found little evidence to support claims that the moral majority had secured an increasing political constituency in these areas (Mueller, 1983). In a broader survey Seymour Martin Lipset and Earl Raab concluded:

> . . . the Americans who turned 'Right' in the last election did not by any means agree with the Moral Majority or New Right programmes. These Americans were not supporting specific political solutions any more than they usually do. They wanted a government that would more demonstrably reflect their *mood*: a more assertive America on the world scene and on the

domestic front a serious campaign to fight inflation and refurbish American industry. That is the extent of their political conservatism. (Lipset and Raab, 1981, p. 31; emphasis in original)

What was of some significance in the United States, as in Britain, was the availability of powerful financial backing for new-right ideas, as Wechsler has argued:

To suggest that the successes of the current no-nothingism are the triumph of a new 'populism' is to minimize the degree to which they are the beneficiaries of affluent sponsorship. Any examination of the financial backing of the major new right enterprises reveals that this must be more accurately characterized as a flowering of 'corporate populism', with special 'moral' issues used as a front for the acquisition of political power by special economic interests. (Weschler, 1980)

The capture of the Conservative Party

If there is little evidence that Thatcher's victory in 1979 reflected the emergence of a growing anti-welfare constituency what of her capture of the Conservative Party? Again the evidence suggests that those who see in this the triumphant emergence of the new right and the rout of traditional Conservatism have exaggerated their case. Certainly Thatcher brought to the leadership of the Conservative Party a very different approach from that which had traditionally been adopted, though it was one which had already been foreshadowed by Edward Heath in the Selsdon period of the 1970-74 Conservative government. What is also clear is that Thatcher's victory did not by any means depend upon a groundswell of support for new-right politics. One leading journalist has commented: 'In particular, I am struck by the virtual unanimity of the people I have talked to on the question of Heath's downfall: monetarism or new ideology was not the major issue in the 1975 Tory leadership election' (Keegan, 1984, p. 61).

If the clue to Mrs Thatcher's emergence as leader does not lie in the realms of ideology then it must be sought elsewhere. Indeed it seems that her victory and the subsequent shift to the right in

the Conservative Party was in some ways fortuitous. Disillusion-
ment with Heath, in the wake of the two Conservative electoral
defeats in 1974, coupled with the animosity provoked amongst
backbench Conservatives by his style of leadership, resulted in
demands for a new Party election. Sir Keith Joseph, the obvious
intellectual leader of the right, had ruled himself out, in part as a
consequence of the reaction to a speech in October 1974 which
appeared to suggest the need for social engineering to control the
number of births among the lower orders. In what *The Times*
described as Sir Keith's 'brief discourse into eugenics' he argued:

> The balance of our population, our human stock is threatened
> . . . a high and rising number of children are being born to
> mothers least fitted to bring children into the world and to
> bring them up, they are born to mothers who were first preg-
> nant in adolescence in social classes four and five . . . They are
> producing problem children, the future unmarried mothers,
> delinquents, denizens of our borstals, sub-normal educational
> establishments, prisons, hostels for drifters. (*The Times*, 21
> October 1974)

Margaret Thatcher stepped into the space left by Sir Keith
Joseph but the key architect of her campaign, Airey Neave, was
on the centre left of the party and had sought to persuade White-
law to run against Heath (see Wapshott and Brock, 1983, p. 124).
The campaign sought not to rally the faithful but to secure the
broadest possible basis of support within the Party: 'Her more
obvious right-wing attitudes were consciously played down.
Neave encouraged her to keep the principal issue of the leadership elections to one about the quality of leadership, not ideology, and to indicate that she was to represent a leadership that
would listen to backbenchers' (*ibid*., p. 128). Even St. John-
Stevas, an exceptionally deliquescent Conservative who voted for
Heath – out of loyalty – on the first round, had joined Margaret
Thatcher's campaign committee when Heath dropped out before
the second (St. John-Stevas, 1984).

Sir Keith Joseph's views merit further attention since they constituted an influential critique of many elements of the postwar
consensus. In the Preston speech Sir Keith argued that inflation
was 'threatening to destroy our society' and advocated strict
control over the money supply as the remedy. He explicitly

acknowledged that the speech could be seen as a criticism of policies pursued by previous Conservative governments, of which he had been a member:

> In general terms you could say that inflation is the result of trying to do too much, too quickly. In more specifically economic terms, our inflation has been the result of the creation of new money – and the consequent deficit financing – out of proportion to the additional goods and services available. (*The Times*, 6 September 1974)

Sir Keith dismissed the possibility of tackling inflation through an incomes policy, though such a policy was supported by the Conservative leadership, and argued that attempts to tackle unemployment through reflation were misconceived. Such attempts simply generate a balance of payments problem with a consequent necessity to adopt deflationary policies again. Reflationary policies also ignored the fact that the unemployment statistics vastly overstated the level of unemployment since they included many who could not really be regarded as unemployed:

> Only when we have deducted all these categories, the frictional – say up to eight weeks between jobs – the unenthusiastic, the unemployable, the fraudulent and the elderly who are obliged to register – do we have the real involuntary unemployment in the Keynesian sense, that is to say people who are both willing and able to work and who have been unemployed for over eight weeks. (*ibid.*)

He also suggested that in any case the problem of unemployment was exacerbated by the rising level of benefits: 'As the scale has risen we have increased the proportion of relatively low earners with large families who would be better off unemployed, and of the many more who would scarcely be any better off if they were at work.' Just as his commitment to 'sound money' as the key to national recovery endorsed a central plank in monetarist economic policy, so his concern about the 'demoralizing influence of our well-intentioned welfare system' reflected another prominent new-right concern.

Sir Keith's speech was widely recognized as constituting a challenge to the thinking of the Conservative leadership. It was described in an enthusiastic *Times* editorial as 'certainly one of the most important political speeches of recent years' (6 September 1974). Some critics expressed concern at what they regarded as Sir Keith's willingness to tolerate significantly higher levels of unemployment, but reaction to the Preston speech was mild compared to the furore created by the second major speech which Sir Keith devoted to social policy.

In a speech in Edgbaston, Birmingham, in which he called for the 'remoralization' of the nation's life, Sir Keith asserted the need to maintain traditional standards of morality and praised 'that admirable woman, Mary Whitehouse ... An unknown middle-aged woman, a schoolteacher in the Midlands, set out to protect adolescents against the permissiveness of our time' (*The Times*, 21 October 1974). He defended the importance of the family:

> The socialist method would take away from the family and its members the responsibilities which give it cohesion. Parents are being divested of their duty to provide for their family economically, of their responsibility for education, health, upbringing, morality, advice and guidance, of saving for old age, for housing. When you take responsibility away from people you make them irresponsible. (*ibid*.)

Sir Keith gave a vigorous endorsement to those who argued that the welfare state promoted dependency amongst its recipients and, whilst consuming ever larger sums of money, failed to fulfill its promise in tackling social problems or improving standards. He linked this to larger claims about the effects of such spending and its malign influence on wider social attitudes. What caused most comment was Sir Keith's suggestion, to which we have already referred, that the nation's 'human stock is threatened'.

The speech was also notable for capturing the increasingly strident if not hysterical mood which dominated many new-right pronouncements in the 1970s. Sir Keith concluded his speech by suggesting that 'this could be a watershed in our national existence. Are we to move towards moral decline reflected and intensified by economic decline, by the corrosive effects of inflation? Or can we remoralize our national life, of which the economy is an integral part?' (*ibid*.).

The sense of an imminent if not immanent crisis pervaded new-right thinking in Britain. A month earlier, in a paper to the

British Association for the Advancement of Science, Samuel Brittan, Economics Editor of the *Financial Times*, had argued that liberal representative democracy was likely to pass away within the foreseeable future because of

> the generation of excessive expectations and the disruptive effects of the pursuit of group self interest . . . It is the competitive bidding for votes among an extensive electorate that distinguishes the democratic system . . . The temptation becomes overwhelming to politicians – the oppositon parties are bound to promise to do better and the government party must join the auction. (*The Times*, 4 September 1974)

This attack on what was seen as ever-growing state involvement particularly in the welfare area was linked to a larger concern about what was seen as the domination of concerns over social justice and egalitarianism: democracy might be saved 'if contemporary egalitarianism were to lose its hold over the intelligentsia' (*ibid.*).

Joseph's speeches established the wider social and economic paradigm for the new-right agenda and undoubtedly reflected as well as helped to mould influential views in the Party. Margaret Thatcher's leadership campaign was not about monetarism but Sir Keith's views nonetheless remained influential.

The simultaneous appeal to old-fashioned moral values and easily understood economic remedies – and who could be against sound money? – appealed to Mrs Thatcher's instincts. She was not by origin or nature a member of that patrician class of Conservatives who have seen politics as, at least in part, concerned with fulfilling the duties and obligations consequent upon privilege. Thatcher was of the *nouveau riche* and while she has been fond of stressing her modest origins in Grantham she has been less assertive about her later life. At the age of twenty-six she married a wealthy businessman, Denis Thatcher, and at the birth of her children, the twins Mark and Carol, they immediately employed a live-in nurse and subsequently nannies. When later they moved to a five-bedroomed mansion in Farnborough they had added a cleaner and a gardener to the staff (Wapshott and Brock, 1983, pp. 60 and 62). When Mrs Thatcher stresses the importance of the family, self-reliance, independence and doing for oneself she does so from the secure, if unacknowledged,

position of wealth. Support for private medicine, private education, private pension provision and the rest may be no more than
an unreflective common sense to those who are millionaires.
Thatcher has argued: 'A man must choose between spending and
saving; between housing himself and depending on the state to
house him at his fellow citizen's expense, between paying for his
children's education and accepting whatever the state provides.'
(Thatcher, 1977, p. 108).

Faith in theory

> What has changed in contemporary society is that the media
> now select and authenticate the really authoritative and influ-
> ential intellectuals ... A new careerist intelligentsia, created
> by, and dependent on, a centralized network of editors, produ-
> cers and presenters – a hired network which is socially and
> politically authoritative because by the facts of ownership and
> control of distribution it is there – is now in command. (Wil-
> liams, 1981)

The answer to the triumphant emergence of monetarism as a
panacea for the nation's ills lies not in the sudden conversion of
Conservative MPs to this doctrine and their consequent election
of Margaret Thatcher or indeed in the conversion of the population at large. Rather monetarism owed its success firstly to its
apparent ability to provide an explanation for Britain's economic
problems and an agenda for action to tackle them. The economic
and social doctrines of monetarism appealed to those hostile to
what they perceived to be the prevailing egalitarian ethos, to
those who were critical of the welfare state and in favour of allowing the successful to keep a greater proportion of the rewards of
their success.

Monetarism may have had little merit as a soundly based
theory of the economy or even of the role of money, but it was
attractively simple. To those without the benefit of any prior education in economics the argument that nations, just like households, had to manage within their budgets was no more than
common sense, even if Keynes had explained why this kind of
sense could have ruinous national consequences. The vivid

imagery of inflation resulting from the overactive printing presses at the Bank of England was easily within the popular grasp. Keynesians struggled to find a solution to slumpflation which appeared to demand contradictory remedies, fuelling demand through tax cuts, or public spending to cure the former whilst curbing demand to control prices. Monetarists had no such dilemmas: control of the money supply, restrictions on public spending and actions to break trade union monopolies would control inflation and secure an economic recovery. Tax cuts would unleash the energies of discouraged entrepreneurs and executives.

Not surprisingly, monetarism had a particular attraction for many of the well heeled but it also attracted important and influential support from sections of the press. William Keegan has argued that 'a crucial role in the ascendancy of monetarist thinking in Britain in the early 1970s was played by the press. The principal economic commentators of both the *Financial Times* and *The Times* during that period – Samuel Brittan and Peter Jay – were disillusioned Keynesians' (Keegan, 1984, p. 41). Not that monetarism was confined to these papers:

> The features, leading articles and political columns of the *Daily Telegraph* and *Daily Mail* were easy converts to the new religion ... monetarism also won over *The Times* editor, William Rees-Mogg; and monetarism and the IEA/CPS approach to life received strong support from Ronald Butt, who wrote on politics regularly for *The Times* and the *Sunday Times*. Even the *Guardian* for a time, gave free vent to monetarism through the pen of Hamish McRae, its financial editor. (*ibid.*, p. 60)

There were no other proposed solutions to Britain's economic problems which either afforded the apparently simple remedies suggested by monetarism or were able to martial so formidable and coherent a body of support. Keynesian remedies appeared to have been overtaken by events; corporatist approaches had also failed to deliver the goods and were in any case antithetical to the individualistic and, more particularly, anti-union ethos of much of the press and Conservative Party. Incomes policies were assailed not only for their ineffectiveness but also for the dangerous supposition that there was some way in which a just determination of wage levels could be made outside the operation of market forces.

Monetarism provided the central rallying point for critics of the postwar consensus and provided an intellectual rationale for those seeking an alternative social vision. Andrew Gamble has drawn attention to the crucial importance of Britain's postwar economic decline in precipitating a break with traditional political remedies (Gamble, 1981). Monetarism promised both higher growth and a more morally rigorous society free from the debilitating effects of excessive welfare. It provided apparently cogent intellectual arguments against income redistribution, unless it were towards upper-income groups, and against powerful trade unions, publicly provided welfare and growing government intervention – except of course in the areas of defence, law and order and those measures required to ensure the supremacy of the market. It was unnecessary for Conservative constituents or even MPs to master the mysteries of the money supply; there were enough themes within monetarism to guarantee a strong resonance with important sections of the Conservative Party.

The press was to continue to play an important role in articulating the new moral, social and economic vision of Thatcherism. It was a vision simultaneously committed to the restoration of nineteenth-century liberalism in economics and the creation of a new nationalistic and authoritarian mood in politics. Indeed whilst the supporters of Hayek and Friedman asserted that their demands for the triumph of market mechanisms were no more than the *sine qua non* of liberty, other voices were already urging that greater freedom need not be the dominant agenda. The *Daily Telegraph*'s Peregrine Worsthorne suggested that:

If one were to probe into the hearts of many potential and actual Tory supporters – and others besides – one might well discover that what worries them most about contemporary Britain was not so much a lack of freedom as its excessive abundance; not so much the threat of dictatorship as the reality of something unpleasantly close to chaos . . . and for Mrs Thatcher to tell a party indignant at the collapse of all forms of authority, and longing for the smack of firm government that the country is suffering from a lack of liberty makes her seem out of touch with reality . . . The urgent need today is for the state to regain control over 'the people'. (Cowling, 1978, p. xx)

The combination of monetarist economics and authoritarian politics was not entirely fortuitous. If the pursuit of monetarist objectives involved attacks on traditional trade union rights, significant increases in the level of unemployment and real reductions in the standards of living of the poorer sections of the population, it was perhaps to be expected that not everyone would share the enthusiasm of the financial journalists. Monetarism's previous forays into the real world, notably in Chile, had at least had the advantage of full military backing.

The prophets of doom who had seen democracy to be threatened and the future of civilization to be at stake in the inflationary spiral of the late 1970s had already created a crusading climate. Under the Thatcher government this was to be continued with an active chorus of support from the press. Indeed monetarism could readily be linked with revivalism, as it was by the *Daily Mail*'s 'distinguished commentator' Andrew Alexander, writing on the dangers of public spending: 'Certainly the economic case for curbs is overwhelming. But there is perhaps an even more important issue a moral one. For high government spending is a fundamental cause of today's decline in moral standards' (*Daily Mail*, 31 November 1983). Invoking the spirit of the Falklands, *Spectator* editor, Charles Moore, found yet another reason to cut back the welfare state:

> The public services are now the main, almost the only base for the power and jobs of the professional Left. Yet they are the only field on which socialist attitudes go unchallenged. Until they capture that field, as they have done with the sale of council houses, the Conservatives will be beaten with the stick of welfare, trying desperately to outdo labour in profligacy in order to stave off disapproval. Such a capture would be no more difficult than the recapture of the Falklands – virtually impossible, yet absolutely necessary. (*Spectator*, 11 June 1983)

Thatcherism essentially linked the authoritarian themes of traditionalist right-wing Conservatives like Worsthorne and

Scruton with the panaceas offered by monetarist advocates, whether journalists or luminaries of the Institute of Economic Affairs. Monetarist economic policies were to be linked with a strong law and order stance, an assertive nationalism and a willingness to appeal to overtly racist sentiments. In 1982 Thatcher's adroit mobilization of jingoistic sentiment and the successful reclaiming of the Falklands were to produce a significant upturn in the Conservatives' popular support. In 1978 a similarly effective use of the emotive issue of race and immigration had produced a parallel upturn. Margaret Thatcher's views on race and immigration first came to prominence in a television interview in late January 1978. This followed racial tension and disturbances involving black and white young people. In the programme, in a premeditated response, Thatcher suggested that people felt 'swamped' by the number of immigrants and that firm action must be taken to control numbers. The impact of the programme is suggested in the fact that Thatcher reportedly received more than 10,000 letters supporting her views (Arnold, 1984, p. 158). In holding out the prospect of an end to immigration, except for compassionate cases, and in bringing popular concerns over race to the fore, Thatcher appeared to galvanize an important sector of electoral opinion 'The Conservative Party moved sharply ahead in the polls at a time when the Conservatives appeared to be losing the initiative to the government' (Layton-Henry, 1978, p. 401).

Race remained prominent in the North Ilford by-election in March which saw a big swing to the Conservatives. In April the Conservatives' new immigration proposals were formally announced, producing this comment in a *Guardian* editorial: 'The package reeks of electoral politics. Every possible "tough" sounding proposal has been dredged up but several of them can only be there for show rather than substance' (8 April 1978). Nonetheless, irrespective of the practical weakness of the Conservative proposals, including the ill-fated undertaking to produce a register of dependants, the Conservatives had for the first time staked a clear claim, from the leadership, for the Powellite vote. An IRN/ORC poll in North Ilford in March claimed that 48 per cent of the voters who switched from Labour to Tory were influenced by the immigration issue (Leigh, 1978).

The election

The Thatcherite rhetoric was strong on the themes of independence, family responsibility, the need to restore incentives and to unleash enterprise. In the field of policy, however, rhetorical flourishes were not matched by specific proposals. In part this was because such proposals could have threatened disunity within the Conservative Party and, perhaps more importantly, because they may well have been perceived as electorally unattractive. To be in favour of tax cuts was one thing; to go to the country on proposals for educational vouchers and the dismantling of the NHS would have been to invite ridicule and defeat.

Behrens divides the Conservatives into Ditchers, 'United in their belief that post-war interventionism, through all its faults, was based on the principles essential for a sound body politic' and Diehards, who saw the key tasks as being 'to reduce the role of the state in society, to divorce politics both from economics and from social policy, and to banish monopoly from the private sector' (Behrens, 1980, pp. 8 and 9). Behrens suggests that one of the clues to Thatcher's early success in uniting the Party is to be found in her deliberate vagueness in the policy area: 'The fervent enunciation of Diehard views . . . was coupled with extreme caution in the area of explicit policy commitment' (*ibid.*, p. 124).

The creation of the right kind of image for the new conservatism and the focus on symbolic rhetoric also fitted in well with the new political marketing strategy being developed. In the years to come Margaret Thatcher was to take lessons which would enable her to project her policies in an uncharacteristically mellifluous tone, to dye her hair, to have her teeth capped and to be carefully groomed for each major TV appearance, usually with an approved interviewer, and often broadcast live only after the most extensive rehearsals. But this concern with product marketing was already evident in the 1979 election. Arnold notes:

> In a manner not previously attempted by the Conservative Party, Margaret Thatcher had cultivated press, radio and television personalities, raised the whole tenor of public relations thinking and devised an overall strategy of advertising and salesmanship unprecedented in British politics . . . The chosen

vocabulary for the important opening paragraphs of the manifesto referred to a Britain that had 'lost its way' and was
'shaken' by a loss of confidence, self respect, commonsense,
'even our sense of common humanity'; society 'seemed on the
brink of disintegration'. (Arnold, 1984, pp. 160-61)

The 1979 electoral manifesto in fact gave little reason for supposing that the Conservatives' policies towards social welfare
would be decisively different. Certainly there was little direct evidence of a monetarist anti-welfare ideology. The key role in
drafting the manifesto had been played by the head of the Conservative research department, Chris Patten, a distinctly deliquescent Conservative. Only the sale of council housing could be
seen as an unequivocal step in the direction of the minimalist
approach to state welfare advocated by monetarists. Significantly this was a broadly popular move, not least because the
manifesto assured those who had been council tenants for three
years a 33 per cent discount on the purchase price, and those who
had been council tenants for longer an even larger discount.
Council house sales hence appealed not only to those who were
ideologically unsympathetic to state involvement in the housing
market, but also to those who stood to obtain a substantial
material gain from purchasing their homes.

The manifesto argued 'The welfare of the old, the sick, the
handicapped and the deprived has also suffered under Labour.
The lack of money to improve our social services and assist those
in need can only be overcome by restoring the nation's prosperity' (Conservative Central Office, 1979, p. 26). In the short term
the Conservatives promised to deploy resources more effectively, not to reduce spending on the Health Service but to decentralize and cut back bureaucracy and hence deliver a better
service to patients.

The Party promised higher standards of education and in particular noted: 'Much of our higher education in Britain has a
world-wide reputation for its quality. We shall seek to ensure that
this excellence is maintained' (*ibid.*, p. 25).

In the area of social security the manifesto suggested a concern
to raise the tax threshold in order to reduce the impact of income
tax on the lower paid. The emphasis on restoring work incentives
was on tax cuts rather than benefit cuts: 'Restoring the will to

work means, above all, cutting income tax. It also involves bringing unemployment and short term sickness benefit within the tax
system . . . the rules about the unemployed accepting available
jobs will be reinforced and we shall act more vigorously against
fraud and abuse' (*ibid.*, p. 27). There was no suggestion that the
earnings-related unemployment benefit would be removed, that
the relative value of many benefits would decline, that rates
would cease to be linked to rising earnings, and there was an
explicit denial that there was any intention to increase the
combined impact of tax and national insurance payments on the
low paid.

Whatever else may be said of Margaret Thatcher's mandate
when she arrived at the door of Number 10 in 1979, it was not a
mandate to cut the welfare state. This was not because of any lack
of sympathy for such an objective amongst Thatcher and her
leading supporters, but rather because of the electoral unpopu-
larity and divisiveness of such proposals. This problem was to
continue to impede progress in dismantling the welfare state.
Privately, leading Thatcherites, such as the new Chancellor of the
Exchequer, Sir Geoffrey Howe, might recognize the need for
benefit cuts and for much faster progress in reducing welfare
expenditures. In public the government were forced to be more
conciliatory. This was evident in their response to the Think
Tank proposals, leaked to the *Economist* (18 September 1982),
which envisaged wholesale restructuring of the welfare state. The
government moved quickly to reassure the electorate of their continuing commitment to the major welfare institutions. In practice
the government were forced to proceed by a continuing erosion
of the real level of benefits and the deliberate under-resourcing of
welfare institutions, which allowed them (for example, in the case
of the Health Service) to claim a continuing commitment whilst
ignoring the impact of demographic shifts and cost inflation.

To the undoubted regret of the leading anti-welfare ideologues
the government strategy appeared to be to erode the welfare state
by attrition rather than to abolish it by full frontal assault.
Nonetheless, as we will see, the Thatcherite record in shifting
resources from health, social services, housing and education to
defence and law and order should not be underestimated. In the
government's first term of office there took place a significant
shift in income in favour of upper-income groups. Indeed, as we

will see, the Thatcher government achieved a greater degree of redistribution in favour of the rich than any of the three previous Labour governments had achieved in favour of the poor. Benefit levels fell, the number living in poverty increased, the wage levels of the poorest sections of the workforce fell relative to those of higher-paid workers, charges were increasingly used to ration welfare resources and to finance their cost, the private sector in health and education expanded, and the quality of state education became increasingly dependent upon the entrepreneurial initiative of teachers and the local PTA.

Poverty and wealth

The attitude of monetarist politicians and publicists towards the issues of wealth and poverty was ambiguous. Sir Keith Joseph, for example, argued:

> By any absolute standard there is very little poverty in Britain today. There are those who, like the old, the disabled, widows and some one-parent families, have special needs. There are other cases of poverty of a kind which no society can entirely eliminate because they result from, say, gross mismanagement, alcoholism or some unforeseen disaster. (Joseph and Sumption, 1979, pp. 27-8)

From this point of view the problem is not really one of poverty but of the way in which the issues of inequality and poverty have been confused. David Marsland, Assistant Director of the new right think tank, The Social Affairs Unit, argues that claims of 'low pay' affecting 'more than six million adult workers mean nothing, absolutely nothing, except that six million workers earn less than the amount arbitrarily defined as acceptable' (Marsland, 1984). The problem, then, lies not in the world but in the operation of the fevered imagination of the sociologist, or worse still of the socialist.

In the United States Martin Anderson of the Hoover Institute, who subsequently became an adviser to President Reagan, was also heralding the abolition of poverty:

> The 'war on poverty' that began in 1964 has been won. The

growth of jobs and income in the private economy, combined with an explosive increase in government spending for welfare and income transfer programmes, has virtually eliminated poverty in the United States. (in Harrington, 1984)

Margaret Thatcher had also drawn attention to the onward march of egalitarianism, noting that between 1911 and 1972 the proportion of wealth owned by the top one per cent of the population (excluding pension rights) had fallen from 69 per cent in 1911 to 28 per cent in 1972. She concluded:

> ... so the fact about economic inequality (as opposed to the myth) is that the rich are getting poorer and the poor are getting richer. This is due both to market forces and government action through the tax system. Taking further money from the rich will no longer make a significant difference to the wealth of the bulk of the population; nor would taxing them more heavily pay for much more government spending; nor would it do much to diffuse economic power more widely. That power is already largely in the hands of government and labour unions. (Thatcher, 1977, pp. 3 and 4)

The fact is of course that the statistics which Thatcher carefully selects tell us only what they tell us. In particular they obscure the way in which, while there was downward wealth redistribution, it remained disproportionately concentrated in the upper-income ranges. As one analysis concluded: 'the distribution that took place was from the very rich to the rich; the poor gained nothing' (*New Society*, 1981, p. 479).

Thatcher further supported her argument by the claim that 'Although the share of the *taxable* income of the poor has not increased to so great an extent they are, nonetheless, markedly better off in relative (as well as absolute) terms than they were before the war' (Thatcher, 1977, p. 3; emphasis in original). This she claimed was a consequence of redistributional welfare programmes. In fact the after-tax share of income of the bottom 20 per cent actually fell after 1949 (Owen, 1981, p. 78). The Royal Commission on the Distribution of Income and Wealth concluded: 'Change has not been very pronounced except at the top; the share of the bottom half has not changed since 1949' (Royal Commission on the Distribution of Income and Wealth, 1980, p. 8).

Thatcher's argument that further redistribution of wealth would make no difference was simply an arithmetical nonsense. Chris Pond of the Low Pay Unit calculated that:

> If the total marketable wealth recorded by the Inland Revenue was shared equally, every member of the adult population would have owned just under £13,000 in 1980 *after* paying all debts, mortgages and liabilities. Half the population had wealth of little more than £1,500 – an eighth of the amount they would have owned in an equal society. By contrast those in the richest one per cent of wealth holders owned, on average, net wealth of almost £300,000 each, or 23 times an equal share, and almost 200 times the amount owned by the poorer half of the population. (Pond, 1982)

Since, in Thatcher's view, there would be no purpose in further wealth redistribution and the lack of progress on income redistribution was compensated for by other factors, the problem was how to explain the continued 'powerful and vocal lobby in Britain to press for greater equality ... Often the reasons boiled down to an undistinguished combination of envy and what might be termed "bourgeois guilt"' (Thatcher, 1977, p. 4).

Others of the new right may not have been so certain about the statistics but had little doubt about the character of the poor. Ferdinand Mount, who served for some time as the head of the Policy Unit at No. 10, has given us the benefit of his investigations: 'The rich admire the poor less and less, partly because the poor are not as poor as they used to be, but also because the poor fritter their money on such trash – video cassettes and cars with fluffy mice that joggle in the back window' (*Spectator*, 20 February 1982).

It is, of course, precisely cars, videos and fluffy mice that represent the triumphant achievement of the free enterprise market. However, the benefits of this market are not shared in quite the manner that Mr Mount imagines. It does seem improbable that the poor own significant numbers of home video machines, unless acquired by unconventional means. The evidence on the relationship between car ownership and social class and income is clear enough though it is possible, in the absence of conclusive counter evidence, that the poor may keep fluffy mice at home.

In fact poverty remained a major problem in both the United

States and the United Kingdom. In the United States Michael Harrington, author of the seminal work on American poverty, *The Other America: Poverty in the United States*, suggested that in 1984 'there are in the range of 40 million to 50 million Americans who live in poverty' (Harrington, 1984, p. 181). Poverty was not just a statistical invention but had an impact on that most fundamental of all issues, life itself:

> In 1975, in Sweden, an infant was much more likely to survive the first year of life than in the United States (there were 8.6 deaths for every 1,000 births in Sweden, 16.1 in this country). Again, the infant mortality rate in the United States for blacks is three times that for Sweden as a whole (24.9 per cent against 8.6 per thousand). (*ibid.*, p. 173)

In the UK the DHSS Black Report found evidence that differences in life expectancy between social classes were actually widening.

The new right have, then, a flexible response to the question of poverty. If it exists it is best tackled by a more rigorous application of market forces, by the dismantling of welfare provision which is a burden on the economy and primarily benefits welfare providers rather than clients, and by the removal of redistributive taxation measures which penalize effort, reduce incentives and consequently slow down economic growth – which together with individual effort constitutes the only real hope for the poor. On the other hand, to those who might argue that such measures are in many ways more of the same, for after all we already have a market-dominated economy in which the rich live qualitatively different lifestyles than the poor, they have a second answer: poverty has by and large already been abolished, hence, not only do we not need any further welfare measures but we can begin to dismantle or reduce many of those we already have.

3. The Thatcher Government

The advent of the Thatcher government coincided with a world recession. The decline in output, the increase in unemployment and continuing inflationary pressures had their effects on the welfare measures adopted and on the wider policy discussions. The economic downturn reduced government revenue while the rapid increase in unemployment increased the size of the social security bill. The government's own commitment to a rapid increase in spending on defence and law and order placed a further pressure on public spending, which rose, as a proportion of GDP, from 49.2 per cent in 1978 to 55.5 per cent in 1981. Social services and social security benefits accounted for 23.2 per cent of GDP in 1978 and 27.4 per cent in 1981 (Unemployment Unit Briefing, 1983). The Institute of Fiscal Studies estimated that the total cost to the Exchequer of unemployment in 1981-82 was £12.9 billion, which in real terms was a 236 per cent increase on the corresponding figure for 1979-80 (*ibid.*).

It would be a mistake to see the government as passive victims of wider recessionary pressures. Rather the pursuit of monetarist policies significantly reduced output and raised the level of unemployment. In comparison with other OECD countries, Britain's inflation rate fell slightly faster – by five per cent between 1979 and 1983, as against four per cent elsewhere. Unemployment, however, increased by 7.8 per cent, as against 3.8 per cent for OECD countries as a whole. In OECD countries as a whole national income rose, while in Britain it fell: taking 1979 as 100, Britain's GNP in 1983 was 97.5 as against an average of 103.4 for OECD countries.

The first budget, in June 1979, saw a cut in the top rate of income tax from 83 per cent to 60 per cent and a reduction in the standard rate of tax from 33 pence in the pound to 30 pence. These cuts in direct taxation were offset by an increase in VAT to

15 per cent and price rises in the nationalized industries, which reduced the requirement for government subsidy or increased the government's profit. The main beneficiaries of these shifts, as of subsequent tax cuts, were the upper-income groups. William Keegan has noted that the monetarists had no expectation that the increase in VAT would affect inflation since they believed this was caused by the money supply rather than by wage pressures. In fact, argues Keegan, the measures gave a marked boost to the inflationary spiral:

> The Thatcher administration presided over a rise in the inflation rate to 21.9 per cent in its first year of office. It devoted the next two and a half years to applying the fiscal squeeze which brought inflation back to the rate which had been inherited. Only during the fourth year did inflation come down below the inherited rate. And during the four years as a whole prices rose on average by over 50 per cent. Unemployment during this period was more than doubled to three and a half million, and manufacturing output fell by a fifth between the second quarter of 1979 and the last quarter of 1980, with no signs of recovery in 1981 or 1982 and the merest glimmer during the spring of 1983. (Keegan, 1984, p. 202)

In the long term the government learned the lesson of experience, that monetary policy was an inadequate tool against inflation. Subsequently, measures were taken to constrain public sector wages, while the rapid increases in unemployment helped limit private sector wage increases. In the short term, however, it is worth recording that such was the new government's commitment to monetarism that ministers could regularly be heard assuring the public that it was ultimately money supply and not trade union demands which caused inflation. This message might have been more welcome at Congress House had its policy implications been less disastrous. What the monetarists argued was that if money supply was properly controlled then those firms which gave wage increases to their workers which were not compensated for by increased productivity would ultimately pay the price of bankruptcy. The consequence of this argument was that incomes policies were not only ideologically offensive in that they demanded government intervention in the market but that they were also economically unnecessary.

The wider economic context within which Thatcherite social policies unfolded is important. The welfare of the population is clearly not simply a consequence of specific welfare measures; it is also a consequence of fiscal policy measures, economic growth and the way in which rewards are allocated in the market. What happened under Thatcherism was that government policies specifically sought to redistribute income towards upper-income groups. At the same time, the rise in unemployment and the consequent pressures on those in work had a particularly adverse consequence on the low paid. This was compounded by the impact of government measures which sought to reduce benefit levels and increase the use of fees and other deterrents to service takeup.

The government's economic policies provided the broad context within which particular social measures unfolded. Monetarism required the adoption of deflationary measures and public sector cutbacks which accelerated the impact of the world recession. Its inevitable consequence was rising unemployment, particularly amongst the low paid.

The deleterious social consequences of monetarism were defended by the argument 'there is no alternative'. This appeal to 'common sense' served to legitimate the unequal nature of the sacrifices demanded in pursuit of the government's economic policy. Keynes, criticizing the monetarist policy of the 1920s, argued that it was 'simply a campaign against the standard of life of the working classes [operating through] the deliberate intensification of unemployment . . . by using the weapon of economic necessity against individuals and particular industries' (Walker, 1983, p. 14).

The income share of the poor declined. Between 1977 and 1981 the share of original income from the labour market of the poorest 40 per cent of households fell from 9.7 per cent to 9 per cent, while the income share of the top fifth rose from 44.5 per cent to 46.1 per cent (Bosanquet, 1983, p. 17). Between 1979 and 1982 the gross pay of the poorest 10 per cent of manual workers increased by 42 per cent, that of the highest 10 per cent of non-manual workers by 63 per cent (*ibid*., p. 18). For the first time in the postwar period the situation of the poor in the labour market actually deteriorated relative to that of other groups.

Specific government measures, notably privatization, also had an adverse effect upon the poor. This occurred as a consequence of the privatization of aspects of public services, notably refuse collection, cleaning and other hospital ancillary services, and also through the privatization of public assets. David Thomas, in a comparison of the consequences of privatization of public companies for the role of unions, found that in general there had been no marked deterioration in attitudes towards pay and consultation. A notable exception was in the British Rail hotels which had been sold off where, in some cases, there had been a marked deterioration in job security, pay and conditions. Thomas argued that this offered

> an important clue about privatisation which has so far been ignored. There's no reason to suppose that privatisation will affect workers in different enterprises in the same way ... the skilled Amersham International workers improve their wages and numbers; the unskilled hotel workers suffer ... Public ownership appears to have raised the pay and conditions of less skilled staff with poor bargaining power (like clerks and some manual workers) and depressed the rewards which skilled workers (like managers and qualified engineers) would expect in the private sector. In this precise sense, it has been an egalitarian force. (Thomas, 1984, p. 179)

The privatization of public assets also brought significant gains to those able to purchase shares. By 1984 those who had bought into British Aerospace or Amersham International and kept their shares had more than doubled their money. Those who bought Cable and Wireless shares at £1.12 could sell them in December 1984 for £4.20. In the same month the four million purchasers of British Telecom shares could double their money almost overnight. This government benevolence served further to enhance the position of those upper-income groups most likely to take advantage of such offers.

Government economic policies which generated rising levels of unemployment amongst the low paid and unskilled meshed with privatization strategies which sought to contract out areas of public service delivery to private firms. The areas initially affected were labour intensive, and the ability of private companies to make savings depended in large measure upon the availability of a pool of labour prepared to work for pay and conditions below those currently afforded to public sector employees doing the same jobs. One limitation on the effectiveness of this strategy lay in the obligation of private sector employees contracting for public sector work to observe the Fair Wages Resolution. This resolution lapsed as a consequence of government action in September 1983. This gave greater freedom to private sector contractors further to undercut wages and conditions in competing for public sector work. The conscious enthusiasm of the government in pursuing this policy was nowhere better illustrated than in the case of the cleaning of government offices. Following the end of the Fair Wages Resolution, government ministries sought to renegotiate the existing contracts with more than six months to run in order to reduce the price of the contract to take account of the lower wages which could now be paid (Stephenson, 1983).

This pursuit of low pay, as an object of government policy, was not simply a reflection of a miserly concern for the public treasury; rather it was quite clearly linked with the broader theme of pricing the workforce back into work. If unemployment was caused by the disincentive effects of excessive benefit levels and the unrealistic wage expectations of many workers, clearly action was required to change the situation. Indeed in 1984 the Chancellor of the Exchequer, Nigel Lawson, in the Mais Lecture, praised the United States recovery and noted that the wage cuts experienced by the American workforce had played a significant role in this. In contrast he regretted the fact that wage levels in the UK had continued to rise (Lawson, 1984, p. 10).

Whatever the government's failure to reduce the general level of wages, its success in increasing the numbers who are low paid was indisputable. On the basis that low pay started at below two-thirds average male earnings, the Low Pay Unit calculated that while in 1979 one in ten male manual workers and two-thirds of female manual workers were low paid, by 1982 one in six male manual workers and three-quarters of female manual workers fell into that category (Walker *et al*, 1983, p. 18). As the number of the low paid rose, so did their contributions in tax and national insurance. In 1979 the proportion of income paid in tax and national insurance contributions for the married low paid amounted to 21.9 per cent; after the 1983 budget this amount increased to 24.2 per cent (Lister, 1983, p. 84).

The new right in Britain had always proclaimed that the burden of high taxation was one reason for Britain's relative economic decline. In particular the concern was with the increasingly progressive effects of taxation and the supposed disincentive effect this had on the work efforts of leading entrepreneurs and managers. In fact an international comparison of tax and employment incomes in 1983-84 showed that Britain had a relatively high rate of taxation on the poor and in comparison a lower rate on the rich.

A married couple with no children and a gross income of £5,000 per year paid 22 per cent of their income in tax and social security contributions in the UK, as compared to 14 per cent in France, 24 per cent in Germany, 25 per cent in the Netherlands and only 9 per cent in the USA. At earnings of £50,000 a year, tax and social security contributions took 45 per cent of income in the UK, 37 per cent in France, 42 per cent in Germany, 57 per cent in the Netherlands and 36 per cent in the USA (Board of Inland Revenue, 1984). Interestingly, the £50,000 per year couple in the entrepreneurial USA paid nearly four times the percentage of income of the £5,000-per-year couple. In contrast, in the UK the richer couple paid only twice the percentage. Nevertheless, the reduction of tax on upper-income groups in the UK singularly failed to produce the economic miracle which should have resulted from their greater efforts.

The consequences of increasing inequality were everywhere apparent, and while Bishops and Conservative Party Chairman occupied themselves with discussions as to exactly how many pairs of shoes the Sunderland poor possessed, a study of 1,000 people on low incomes found that 37 per cent of the unemployed had had to go without a meal in the last year because they did not have enough money to buy food (Driver, 1984). The report suggested not only that those on low incomes frequently had insufficient to eat but that their diet was often scarcely adequate to maintain good health. Contrary to the general belief that the poor failed to eat nutritionally because of ignorance it was suggested that many in the survey were aware of nutritional arguments about different foods but were not always able to follow them. In the words of one food expert, they were 'unable to follow the developing official consensus about "what is good for you" ... because another consensus elsewhere in Westminster and Whitehall denies them the income they need to eat healthily' (Driver, 1984).

Undoubtedly the most important factors affecting the status and number of the poor can be found in the areas of macroeconomic and taxation policy. The government also took specific measures in the social security field designed to distinguish more clearly between the deserving and undeserving poor, to increase work incentives by reducing the real value of unemployment benefits, to deter and stigmatize claimants and to control costs to the public exchequer. The control of costs was particularly important in the context of the demand-led rise of social security expenditure, which was consequent both upon the government's economic policies and upon demographic changes which were increasing the number of the elderly in the population.

The government's much proclaimed commitment to controlling public spending served to justify cutbacks in health and social services. These cutbacks were more than offset by commitments to increased spending on defence, which rose by 22 per cent in the first seven years, and on law and order. Social security spending, as we have noted, also increased as a consequence of growing unemployment. The net result was an actual increase in the level of public spending, which rose from 40.5 per cent of national income in 1978-79 to 43.5 per cent in 1981-82 before falling back to 41 per cent in 1985-86. In fact the government's practice of counting asset sales as a reduction in expenditure, in spite of criticisms from the House of Commons Treasury and Civil Service Select committee, meant that the real increase in public expenditure was larger than these figures suggest.

4. Impoverishment by Stealth: Social Security Changes in Retrospect

The first Thatcher government used a variety of tactics to reduce the general level of benefits available. Sometimes cuts were made by changing the basis of entitlement, as in the abolition, in 1980, of exceptional needs payments, previously available for the purchase of shoes and clothing; the ending of the earnings-related unemployment supplement or the de-indexing of long-term benefits from movements in wages. Other changes, more characteristic of the government, consisted of manoeuvres designed to reduce the cost of benefits without overtly introducing cuts. Simultaneously the government sought to redefine the terms of entitlement to benefit and, for those who remained entitled, to provide increasing deterrents to takeup. Finally the government sought to privatize aspects of social security in order to achieve a reduction in administrative costs and as part of a wider move to shift the focus of welfare provision from the state to the individual and the market place.

During the first three years of the Thatcher government the number of people dependent on supplementary benefit rose 50 per cent, to 6.5 million by mid-1982. By 1984 more than seven million were dependent on supplementary benefit.

The abolition of the earnings-related unemployment supplement affected only a minority of the unemployed; nonetheless, for this group it was a significant factor, amounting to some £11 per week in 1982. The de-indexing of long-term benefits from the movement in earnings has continuing implications for the relationship between those dependent upon state benefits and the rest of the population. As earnings continue to rise so the gap between those drawing pensions or other benefits and those in work will widen. Indeed in the 1983 election campaign the Conservatives refused to make any commitment to maintain even the link with prices, except in the case of retirement pensions. For the government, the attraction of de-indexing lies not only in the immediacy of the savings to be made, estimated at £500 million per year by 1982-73 (Riddell, 1983, p. 140), but in the way in which the basis of entitlement is eroded. If the gap between those in receipt of state benefits and those in work or covered by private schemes can be steadily increased, state welfare will more closely approximate the residual model of last resort advocated by monetarists. In de-indexing future upgradings from any movement in wages, the government made an important ideological statement which simultaneously paved the way for a continuing relative decline in the value of benefits. For a government committed to dismantling state welfare the attractiveness of this proposal was obvious.

Faced with electoral hostility to a wide-ranging attack on benefit levels the government also sought to erode the value of benefits by more devious means. If frontal assault would precipitate outrage, not only from the Opposition but also from sections of the Party's own backbenchers, then the erosion of benefits at the margins and the use of a sleight of hand which had much in common with mendacity could be employed. This was well illustrated in the Social Security (No. 2) Act of 1980, which introduced a five per cent abatement of unemployment benefit, pending its taxation, which happened in July 1982. Taxation of unemployment benefits not only promised to reduce the net cost to the Exchequer but also fitted in with a wider desire to ensure that the unemployed were worse off than those in work. This in turn would improve work incentives, though in the context of massive increases in unemployment the logic of reducing the living conditions of the unemployed, in order to increase their enthusiasm for work, was not always clear. In fact the introduction of taxation did not result in the restoration of the abatement. This was restored only after backbench Conservative pressure over a year later, in November 1983.

A similar streak of meanness and a willingness to adopt somewhat circuitous routes characterized the government's effort to impoverish not only the unemployed but also the children of all claimants. Claimants' children receive support from child benefit and from national insurance children's additions. The government not only failed to maintain the value of child benefit but it also significantly cut the real value of the national insurance children's addition. As a result total child support over a three-year period declined by 23 per cent for short-term beneficiaries and 12 per cent for long-term beneficiaries. The crucial relationship between child benefits and NI additions was deliberately obscured so that few appreciated the scale of the erosion which had taken place. Fimister aptly summarizes the key to the government's success:

> The government has relied, politically, on the sheer complexity of this manoeuvre in order to get away with it. Efforts by the 'poverty lobby' to raise the alarm have fallen flat, simply because it is so difficult to express the issue in a form digestible to the media and the general public. Meanwhile, the government has audaciously claimed that it is achieving the laudable objective of absorbing NI additions into child benefit. (Fimister, 1983, p. 34)

The government not only achieved a reduction in the general level of benefits but it also achieved significant savings by resisting proposals for change. This was most notable in the case of the government's continuing refusal to improve the position of the unemployed by granting them entitlement to the long-term supplementary benefit rate.

Unemployment benefit lasts for only one year, and growing unemployment resulted in an increasing number of the unemployed becoming dependent on supplementary benefit. The number unemployed for more than a year rose from some 228,000 in 1980 to 779,000 in 1982, then to one million by 1984. In addition, the considerable increase in the number of under-20s who were unemployed – most of whom did not have the necessary contribution record to receive unemployment benefit – also affected the number of unemployed dependent on supplementary benefit. The dramatic increase in youth unemployment is reflected in the fact that by 1984 there were more under-20s claiming benefit, through unemployment, than there were claimants of all ages in 1979 (Lewis, 1984). In the face of overwhelming evidence that unemployment was escalating and that the number of long-term unemployed was increasing rapidly, the government refused to close the gap between short-term and long-term rates. In 1983 the gap amounted to 27 per cent for a single householder and 25 per cent for a couple.

The reasons for the government's refusal were twofold. Firstly, the very escalation of unemployment, which pushed the issue to the forefront of the agenda, guaranteed that any change would be expensive. Second, any improvement in the benefit entitlement of the unemployed would have run directly counter to the government's policy of pricing the unemployed back into work. The government's ideologues, far from being concerned at the inadequacy of short-term benefit levels, were repeatedly warning the government that at existing benefit levels work disincentive effects were so powerful that they would affect even those families with four children and an annual income of £10,400 (Ashton, 1984). Such claims, however, were notably lacking in supporting evidence.

Many of the government's measures consisted of steps intended to reduce expenditure by introducing delays before claimants were eligible and by erecting barriers in the way of those who wished to pursue claims. Obscure rule changes could be brought into play to erode further the living standards of claimants. In 1983 the government changed the basis for calculating future benefit increases: they were now calculated on the basis of the annual rate of inflation in the spring rather than on the basis of the projected increase in the cost of living over the next year. This resulted in an increase of 3.7 per cent being announced, to take effect in November of that year, although the government admitted that it was expected that inflation would in fact increase from 3.7 per cent to 6 per cent. The government claimed that any increase would automatically be taken into account in the following year but, as the Labour MP George Foulkes pointed out, by that time many pensioners would have died and would take little comfort from any future increase (*Guardian*, 24 March 1983).

In another penny-pinching gesture, Dr Rhodes Boyson, the Social Security Minister, admitted to MPs in 1984 that as a consequence of a change in a social security regulation called the 'available scale margin', the government had increased from 50 pence to £1 the amount of money which it was entitled to 'claw back' from people receiving long-term levels of supplementary benefit who also qualified for extra allowances to cover special diets and laundry. The effect of the changes was that some 400,000 people would receive 50 pence per week less and 1.4 million between 50 pence and £1 less (*Guardian*, 23 June 1984).

The young unemployed were also targetted for government cuts. The provisions of the 1980 Social Security (No. 2) Act excluded school leavers from any entitlement to benefit in their own right for up to twelve weeks after leaving school. In April 1983 the £3.10 non-dependant's housing addition was removed from sixteen- and seventeen-year-olds and, in April 1984, it was removed from eighteen- to twenty-year-olds.

The government's obsessive concern with chiselling away at the edges of an already inadequate benefit structure was again demonstrated in the announcement, in June 1984, that claimants would have to wait not the customary fifty-two weeks but rather fifty-three weeks before receiving the annual increase in pensions and other benefits.

The government also announced that it would save an estimated £17 million in 1985 by delaying payment of unemployment benefits by one week. Instead of the existing system, where claimants received payment one week in arrears and one week in advance, all new claimants from January 1985 would be paid two weeks in arrears.

In another rule change the government altered the basis on which family income supplement was up-rated. Previously people claiming FIS received an increase at the time of the benefit up-rating in November. In 1984, however, the government determined that the increase would not be available until their current award had ended. Some claimants would therefore wait up to fifty-two weeks before receiving an award which was intended to cover the increased cost of living over that period. A typical two-child family could thus find by this ministerial sleight of hand that they had lost £115 over a year (Lynes, 1984).

The government's energy was devoted not only to finding ways of eroding the living standards of claimants but also to ensuring that any attempts to reverse this process or to use established appeals mechanisms to secure decisions favourable to claimants were defeated. When a Bristol man won a claim for the purchase of an orthopaedic mattress because of severe back trouble, he established on appeal before three social security commissioners a precedent for other disabled people living on benefits to make similar claims. Within forty-eight hours Rhodes Boyson placed a new regulation before Parliament halting any further payments, and had it passed into law (*Guardian*, 23 November 1983). In

March 1984, in a case taken by CPAG on behalf of a client, the Social Security Commission ruled that holiday pay payments in lieu should be calculated in such a way as to make claimants eligible almost as soon as they left work, rather than, as had often been the case, having to wait until such income was assumed to be exhausted. Again Dr Boyson immediately moved to put emergency regulations through the House of Commons effectively to nullify the decision (*Guardian*, 21 March 1984).

One set of cuts about which the government made no secret was the introduction in the 1980 Social Security (No. 2) Act of a deduction from the entitlement of families of strikers of £14.50, assumed to represent the contribution from the breadwinner's strike pay. This was followed by the announcement, in the midst of the miners' strike, that any payment in kind to claimants, including the value of groceries, firewood or other gifts, should be deducted from claimants' benefit entitlement (*Guardian*, 16 May 1984).

Policing the poor

Parallel with these changes to claimants' entitlements went a more determined attempt to stigmatize those dependent on benefits. In pursuit of the ever-present goal of reducing the number of public sector employees, the government cut back the number of social security staff, in spite of the very large increase in the number of claimants. The only area in which a significant increase of staff took place was in the number of those employed on social security fraud.

Cutbacks in the number of social security staff in local offices made it difficult for claimants to register, seek advice and secure their full entitlement. For example, between 1980 and 1982 it was estimated that the workload in DHSS offices in Merseyside increased by 70 per cent, yet during the same period staff were cut. According to a report from the Society of Civil and Public Servants some 100,000 potential claimants in the area were not taking up their supplementary benefit and £17 million in potential benefits was unclaimed. Hundreds of visits to claimants which could have resulted in additional payments for heating or special diets had to be cancelled (*Guardian*, 9 October 1982). In the Midlands the number of social security staff was cut by 14 per cent while their workload was estimated to have increased by 25 per cent (*ibid*.). Given the large number of people who are entitled to claim benefit but do not do so, the degree of openness and access to the benefits system is important. At the end of 1983 the Social Security Minister, Rhodes Boyson, released figures which indicated that only two in three of those eligible were claiming supplementary benefit (*Guardian*, 3 December 1983). Even those who did claim could not rely on receiving a full consideration of their entitlement. Research carried out by the Policy Studies Institute found that DHSS staff were often misinformed and that six out of seven of those interviewed said they were under too much work pressure to give each task enough attention (Policy Studies Institute, 1984).

A research paper by Henkel and Pavelka from the Vienna-based European Centre for Social Welfare, which looks at policy and procedures across a range of countries, suggests that the organization of the benefits system and the attitudes expressed within it will have a crucial effect on take-up. In contrast to the assumptions of the new right that claimants are both well informed and vigorous in their pursuit of their entitlement, it is suggested that the interaction between claimants and the benefit system is more complex:

The assumption seems to prevail that the client, armed with comprehensive information, well versed and pugnacious in dealings with official departments, has sallied forth to 'extort' the maximum of social benefits from an absolutely defenceless administration, to exploit legislation to the full and if necessary to resort to illegal practices. In fact, however, the inter-action between applicants and official departments is probably more like a 'bargaining process' – or in other words involves a 'negotiable element'... In a political environment that is 'economy-minded' and attuned to 'combating abuse', there is probably no need for written instructions to induce the staff of welfare offices to observe the principle that 'good management means turning down as many applications as possible'. The rigid observance of this 'guiding principle' can without question have the result that persons who are in fact entitled to benefits fail to take the hurdle of official defense mechanisms and do not receive their due benefits. (Henkel and Pavelka, 1982, p. 5)

In the British context, not only were staff under increasing bombardment from claimants but there was also a growing campaign against alleged scroungers. This came to a head in a widely publicized raid in Oxford in September 1982, which resulted in the arbitrary and often illegal detention of 283 claimants, of whom 179 were subsequently charged.

The Oxford raid made headlines in many national papers, not least because the police claimed to have uncovered a £1½ million fraud. In fact the resulting prosecutions concerned amounts totalling less than £20,000 (*Guardian*, 4 January 1983), as against the estimated £180,000 cost of the operation (*Guardian* letters, 7 February 1983). No charges were brought against any of the landlords who made many thousands of pounds out of accommodating claimants and whose addresses were used for the purpose of drawing benefit. Understaffing at the Oxford office of the DHSS meant that accommodation used for homeless claimants was rarely visited and that no effective action had been taken, despite a warning from Oxford Cyrenians seven years earlier that they suspected that a lodging-house racket was operating in the city (Coulter, 1982). The actions of those prosecuted in Oxford were not, as the police tried to suggest, the product of some massive and devious fraud. Rather, such actions were a direct consequence of the total inadequacy of the current benefits system and the government's failure to tackle the housing needs of the single homeless. These factors, however, did not deter the Oxford magistrates from imposing savage sentences on the accused, even though for many this was a first offence. (One claimant who was found guilty had in fact left the boarding house to visit his sick mother; because of these mitigating circumstances he received a reduced sentence of twenty-one days. In fact, as it subsequently transpired, the DHSS did not even require him to advise them of an absence of such a short duration.) Other claimants received ninety-day sentences (Franey, 1983, p. 36).

The treatment of those who were arrested by the Thames Valley Police would have produced a national outcry had it happened to more affluent citizens. Some of those arrested were not claimants but had gone to the office with a friend who was making a claim.

Those arrested were not advised of their rights and none of the 179 people charged saw a solicitor before going to the courts. Many had bail denied in spite of the fact that this was a first offence of a relatively trivial nature. A young man who refused to be photographed, as was his right, was kept in a police cell over-night before being released without charge. Another youth, again not a claimant, was held for ten and a half hours. One of the claimants, Walter Byrne, who had in fact been sleeping at one of the suspect bed and breakfast addresses, was held in prison with-out bail for twenty-one days before being released by the courts on the grounds that he had no case to answer. Before Operation Major, homeless people requiring urgent-needs payments had had to wait for up to a week before being seen by staff. As a con-sequence of Operation Major a ministerial order was made that all urgent need cases should be seen that day. The additional pressure which this placed on the Oxford DHSS office led to a spontaneous strike by 110 of the 145 staff (*Guardian*, 18 October 1982).

The enthusiastic media response to what it quickly termed Operation Sting, contrasted oddly with the earlier response to dawn raids made by Inland Revenue officials investigating alleged tax frauds (Golding and Middleton, 1982, p. 99). Police claims about the scale of the Oxford fraud subsequently proved to be without foundation, but the media raised no questions as to why it had proved necessary to use large numbers of Alsatian dogs, to deny the accused access to solicitors, to detain those against whom there was no evidence of criminal activity, or indeed to use police for what was usually a matter handled by DHSS investigation staff (Franey, 1983). No doubt for the government it was fortunate that as unemployment continued to rocket public attention should be so forcefully directed to the legendary figure of the social security scrounger.

The mythical £1½ million fraud in Oxford contrasts with the dawn raid against some of those associated with the Rossminster Group not simply in the way in which the media treated the two events. In the Rossminster case the Attorney-General, Sir Michael Havers, decided not to bring charges. The amount involved, however, vastly exceeded even the wildest estimates of the sums involved in Oxford. The *Observer* reported in April 1984 that the Inland Revenue had served estimated tax assessments on Roy

Tucker and Ronald Plummer, the two key figures behind the Group, of up to £16 million each. In addition the Revenue was reported to be pursuing separate tax assessments against others who had been involved, including Tom Benyon, the former Tory MP for Abingdon, in whose constituency Operation Sting had, ironically, taken place (*Observer* Business, 8 April 1984). The *Observer* had earlier reported that the assessment against Mr Benyon alone approached £1.5 million (19 February 1984).

The claim that government sought to deter claimants from taking up their entitlement is not based on the proposition that government ministers actually meet to plan staff reductions as a way of increasing the deterrence to take-up. Rather, what is involved is a general hostility to the welfare benefit system combined with exaggerated beliefs about public sector overstaffing and inefficiency and the prevalence of abuse. The government policies which follow from these beliefs have had the necessary effect. By 1984 the number of people claiming supplementary benefit had risen from three million a week in 1979 to 4.6 million a week. During the same period social security staff increased by a little more than 1,000, with most of them joining the specialist claims-control units to deal with fraud.

In Birmingham, the pressure on the DHSS office resulted in a prolonged strike. The catalyst for the strike, which was to last from September 1982 to May 1983 and to close all eleven DHSS offices in Birmingham, was the collapse of a young civil servant at the Erdington office. She had arrived at work to find that her two fellow receptionists were off and that eighty people were already queueing for service. The strike could not, however, be seen as unexpected; the government had been under pressure for months from civil service unions, the West Midlands County Council and backbench MPs to take action over staffing levels in DHSS offices, particularly those in the Birmingham area where a dramatic increase in unemployment had taken place. Prior to the strike the government had already introduced new regulations providing for emergency payments. This meant that during the course of the strike in Birmingham claimants received a flat rate of benefit which amounted, for example, for a single parent with four children, to £24 per week. A married couple with children received £40 per week. What this meant is illustrated by the case of one claimant who before the strike was receiving £110 per week for his wife and three teenage children and who subsequently received only £40 per week in emergency payments (Coetzee, 1983, p. 37).

Failure to take any action over the earlier warnings of the impending collapse of the social security system in Birmingham, the miserly nature of the emergency payment scheme, the government's unwillingness to take effective action to end the strike and the subsequent continuing delays in dealing with claimants in Birmingham, speaks volumes about the government's attitude to welfare recipients. Months after the strike had ended, claimants in Birmingham were still awaiting payment of outstanding benefits whilst being hounded by public and private landlords and the electricity and gas boards for the payment of outstanding bills. In Operation Major, claimants were denied the basic legal rights and protections formerly guaranteed to all British citizens. In Birmingham claimants were denied the right to those benefits apparently guaranteed by Parliament.

In the meantime, pressure on social security claimants and on DHSS staff continued to mount. Reports suggest that pressure on counter staff dealing with claimants was such that it resulted in an annual 30 per cent wastage rate (*Guardian*, 27 April 1985). Staff at a benefit office near Victoria Coach Station in London, for example, went on strike after the stabbing of one claimant by another. The office, used by many of those who took the government's advice to look for work more energetically by travelling, was under such pressure that up to 300 claimants at a time were waiting for more than seven hours in a waiting room designed to hold forty-five. Single parents with small children were obliged to wait all day for an interview and might still leave without having been seen (*ibid.*).

Deterrents to take-up, whether in the form of increasingly complex benefit regulations, inadequately staffed offices or campaigns of public stigmatization of claimants, were not the only weapons in the government's armoury. Those who presented themselves at benefit offices might be arbitrarily denied benefit, as reportedly happened to some claimants in Oxford (Franey, 1983), or required to overcome a further series of hurdles before benefit was granted. Such hurdles could prove insurmountable. One such case was that of Mr Francis Wharton. Mr Wharton had sought to claim invalidity benefit, which is higher than the short-term unemployment benefit. This claim was supported by his own doctor, but he was also required to attend a Department of Health examination. He was then told to attend a further medical examination and he died on the way. His case was subsequently taken up by his MP after his widow claimed that his death had been caused by the strain brought about as a consequence of these procedures (*Guardian*, 10 October 1983).

The government's concern to police social security fraud was reflected in its appointment of an additional 1,050 social security investigators. Within two years the number of those prosecuted for failing to maintain their alleged dependants had increased from 980 to 2,360 (Novak, 1984, p. 43). In 1981 the 'non-prosecution interview' was introduced. This was a device to be used for getting claims withdrawn on a voluntary basis where insufficient evidence existed to justify prosecution. Not surprisingly, concern was expressed that some claimants would be pressured into withdrawing by the implicit threat of prosecution, in spite of the validity of their claim.

In a parallel move the Employment Secretary, Norman Tebbit, set up a Regional Benefit Investigation Team to persuade suspect claimants to stop drawing unemployment benefit. On the basis of statistical calculations that suggested that the minister was not simply ignorant of the potentialities of the modern bicycle but also of the basics of mathematics, he subsequently claimed savings of over £1 million. This was done on the assumption that each claimant who had withdrawn would not claim benefit for an additional year. In fact many claimants may apply almost immediately – particularly since there is reason to suppose that some of those who withdraw claims have nonetheless a valid and legal basis for their claim. The estimate of the scale of savings was, however, important, since the exercise itself had cost the Department some £307,000, including an expenses bill of nearly £100,000 shared between thirty people (*Guardian*, 27 September 1983).

In spite of the somewhat unpromising rate of return on investment in policing social security and unemployment benefit fraud, the government showed more enthusiasm for staff increases in this area than it did in the vastly larger area of tax fraud. The estimated loss through fraud in the social security system was £100 million; income tax evasion alone is reputed to cost between

£1,000 million and £4,000 million, and unpaid Value Added Tax (VAT) to cost a further £250 to £1,000 million per annum (Levi, 1982, p. 37). Another indication of the size of the tax fraud problem is provided by a contrast with the 1981 Home Office figure for total losses from theft, burglary and robbery in England and Wales: these amounted to £551 million in 1980 (*ibid*.). In contrast to the estimated social security fraud of £100 million, it was estimated in 1979 that there were £572 million of unclaimed benefits on the main means-tested schemes, supplementary benefit, Family Income Supplement, rent rebates and allowances, rate rebates and free school meals (Deacon and Bradshaw, 1983).

Estimates for the rate of return on the employment of additional Inland Revenue staff vary; extra officers are said to bring in somewhere between four and eighteen times their salary (Levi, 1982, p. 36). The Inland Revenue Staff Federation claim that there is a net return in taxes collected of £92,000 for each extra investigating inspector employed. Certainly the data suggest very considerable scope for improved detection and prosecution. The annual report for the Inland Revenue published in 1984 showed that 90 per cent of those companies whose accounts were investigated had understated their profits. Some 37 per cent of companies examined were subjected to penalties in addition to being taxed on the higher profits discovered. Yet fewer than two per cent of the companies were investigated (*Guardian*, 19 July 1984).

The Thatcher government in fact reduced the number of employees in the Inland Revenue by over 12,000. Four hundred VAT control posts were cut though, as the Labour MP Alan Williams argued:

> Over half of those who pay VAT will not have been visited within the three years during which they have to keep their records. Thus, they will not be visited before they are entitled to destroy their records. This is despite the fact that one in three of the checks have revealed underpayment. (*Guardian*, 4 November 1983)

The mounting pressure of work on the Revenue meant increasing delays in handling correspondence. In July 1983 there were five million letters awaiting reply. There was also a 36 per cent increase in tax office arrears from July 1982 (*ibid*.).

At the end of 1983 Tony Christopher, General Secretary of the

Inland Revenue Staff Federation, in response to government plans further to reduce the number of employees in the Revenue, announced that the amount of outstanding tax had reached £718 million. A large amount of this was the PAYE contributions of the employees of small companies whose owners were no doubt enjoying the use of this tax income (*Guardian*, 18 November 1983).

A further illustration of the government's differential treatment of social security fraud and tax fraud is revealed in the number of prosecutions, which again were in total contrast to the relative size of the frauds. In 1980-81 the number of prosecutions brought for social security fraud was 23,767 (Avery, 1982). In 1979 the Inland Revenue prosecuted only 184 tax defrauders (Novak, 1984, p. 44).

The Thatcher government were content to erode further the regulatory activities of government bodies. They presided over a situation in which homeless claimants who committed petty frauds against an inadequate and overworked benefit system would be harassed and jailed and where the well-healed clients and architects of massive tax avoidance schemes could be sure of a sympathetic hearing if their sleep were disturbed by investigating officers from the Revenue at seven in the morning. Michael Levi has contrasted the treatment of tax avoiders with others in the criminal justice system:

> It remains the case that there is a stark contrast between, on the one hand, the routine prosecution of 'ordinary' criminals for offences of often trivial monetary value and, on the other, the extremely low prosecution rate of the Inland Revenue and, pace the Law Society, of HM Customs and Excise. Moreover, the directors of Rossminster who were awakened at 7 a.m. may expect little sympathy from the normal 'clients' of the police, who are inconvenienced at far more unpleasant hours with little technical justification. (Levi, 1982, p. 50)

The treatment of those who avoid tax and those who defraud the social security system provides an even more marked contrast. The Thatcher government did not create this divide, but under the government's aegis the disparity between the two became distinctly more apparent.

The government's enthusiasm for increasing social security investigations can be further contrasted with its parsimony in other areas. In 1979 there were 952 factory inspectors in Britain;

by 1983 the number had been reduced to 852. During the same period the Health and Safety Executive had its staff cut by 700, in spite of the fact that only five per cent of workplace accidents are investigated (Williams, 1983).

Delegation and privatization

In addition to the cutbacks and restrictions already identified, the government also sought to withdraw from direct involvement in providing various benefits through delegation of responsibility to local authorities or private employers. The government's withdrawal from specific areas of provision enabled it simultaneously to reduce the number of civil servants and to deflect both expectations and administrative problems onto other bodies.

The Social Security and Housing Benefits Act 1982 transferred most of the supplementary benefit housing support responsibilities to local authorities. The intention of the Act was to simplify and integrate the various forms of rent support available. The government had been advised by David Donnison, former Chairman of the Supplementary Benefits Commission, that the new scheme could not be introduced in an equitable manner without some increase in public spending. In contrast, the government was committed to a no-cost reform and this commitment, coupled with the government's insensitivity and intransigence, in the face of the problems which rapidly appeared, was responsible for what one expert described as 'the largest administrative shambles of the post-war welfare state' (Weir, 1984B, p. 140).

In its enthusiasm for shedding 2,400 civil servants, the government failed to prepare an alternative system of local administration for housing benefits, leaving local authorities beseiged by claimants and unclear of the rules. A report on the scheme from the National Association of Citizens Advice Bureaus concluded: 'The overall picture is one of operational defects the scale and effects of which can only be described as devastating' (quoted *ibid*.). The primary victims of this shambles, as of the government's other adventures in the social security field, were the weakest members of society. In a graphic description of the administration of housing benefits in Hackney, Stuart Weir detailed the human suffering involved in the long delays which claimants faced before benefit was received. These delays could lead to claimants not only running into debt, in some cases for the first time in their lives, but also being threatened with eviction and having gas and electricity cut off. The pressure on the council office in Hackney was so great that queues started to form two or three hours before it opened. The effect of such queueing was to add to the stigma and demoralization of the claimants. Weir reports an eye-witness account:

> Tony has queued three times now. The first time an old man who was first in the queue – 'he'd been there since 7.30 a.m.' – suddenly squatted down and shat on the pavement. He then wiped himself on a newspaper and threw it into the gutter. He was simply desperate not to lose his place. 'I wasn't at first aware of what was happening. There was this foul smell, and these women in front of me holding their noses and complaining. It was degrading for the old man, and degrading for all of us. I could try and stand back from it and regard it as an experience, but in truth I've also felt, "Christ, have I come down to this so soon? It really is horrifying, standing in the queue."
> (Weir, 1984A, p. 101)

Undeterred by the chaos and hardship already unleashed, the government in November 1983 announced a £230 million package of cuts in housing benefit, further complicating the scheme and indeed revealing its own ignorance of it: it subsequently became clear that three times as many claimants would be affected by cuts as the government claimed when the cuts were first announced (*Guardian*, 1 December 1983).

All that remained was for the Comptroller and Auditor General to report that the new scheme was more costly to administer than the range of benefits that it had replaced. In 1984 a report on the scheme estimated that whereas DHSS staff savings were of the order of 2,400, the additional staff required by local authorities to administer the scheme was in excess of 2,500 (Comptroller and Auditor General, 1984). The government could still, however, seek some reassurance from the fact that a potentially contentious welfare issue had been devolved from central government to local authorities, which had to struggle to administer such new obligations in the context of ever-tighter control over their spending.

The government's proposals for reform of the sickness benefit and sick pay provisions were intended to place the major responsibility for the administration of the scheme on private employers, who would be compensated for their payments out of a reduction in their national insurance contribution liability. The advantage of the scheme was intended to be the integration of national insurance and employer sickness benefits. The government also made the new statutory sick pay liable to income tax and national insurance contributions, with the intention of effecting a net reduction in government spending. In order to simplify the administration of the scheme, no provisions were to be made for family status, hence those with dependants would receive a reduced wage while sick and no allowances for dependants. One effect of the scheme was thus to reduce the level of sick pay for many of the lower paid. The government's capitulation to demands from employers for a more substantial compensation in fact reduced the amount saved by the reform. O'Higgins has argued that in effect much of the revenue raised from taxing sick pay 'funded an income transfer from employees to employers' (O'Higgins, 1984, p. 135). The efficiency of the new privatized scheme is suggested by a survey which found that in 23 per cent of cases checked, employers had underpaid or overpaid (Poverty, 1984, p. 3).

The new scheme, when launched, succeeded in cutting only half the number of civil service jobs claimed and only £40 million off the public sector borrowing requirement, as compared to the £200 million initially proposed (O'Higgins, 1984). The cost of these minor gains was borne by the sick, particularly those with large numbers of dependants and those whose employers might find in the new scheme an incentive to weed out their less robust employees.

In general claimants proved unsuccessful in resisting government schemes to erode entitlement or to change the method under which assistance was administered. One group, however, no doubt because of their degree of public legitimacy, did resist moves towards privatization. A proposal to hive off the government's welfare service for badly disabled war veterans and their widows and orphans to a private or voluntary organization led to protests from the main veterans organizations including the RAF Benevolent Fund and the Royal British Legion. The government's reasoning for the change, which was intended to save an estimated £2.3 million, was disarmingly candid:

> ... the government's wish is that the state should not be undertaking any function which can be done as well, or possibly even better, by the private or voluntary sectors. This is consistent with the aim of reducing the number of civil servants and disengaging the state from any activity which civil servants need not perform. (*Guardian*, 24 November 1981)

In part the savings were to be achieved by limiting the number of visits only to those judged to be in real need. In the face of protests in this politically sensitive area the government ultimately withdrew its proposals.

In general, as David Donnison has argued, claimants are afforded less respect and consideration than other citizens:

> Customers for the services dealing with the poor are given less chance to influence their policies and practices than those relying on other services. Social work and social security are the only major social services still making no systematic attempt to represent and listen to their users. That is because both deal largely with the poor. (Donnison, 1984, p. 17)

The war veterans at least were able to compensate for the stigma of dependency by the patriotic aura which necessarily surrounded that dependency, particularly in a climate where government-fostered jingoism was a powerful force.

Conclusion

The government's policy on social security is clearly an evolving one. The announcement in 1984 of a broad review of social security spending confirmed the government's continuing interest in further cuts in this area. The composition of the new review held little reassurance for claimants. The Children and Young Persons Review Committee, for example, was chaired by Dr Rhodes Boyson, with two independent members, Barbara Shenfield, Chairman of the Women's Royal Voluntary Service, which is entirely funded by the Home Office, and Mr Parry Rogers, Director of Personnel for Plessey and a member of the Institute of Directors. Mrs Shenfield is a well-known new rightist and contributor to an Adam Smith Institute report on social security which advocated wide-scale dismantling and privatization of existing social security provision (Adam Smith Institute, 1984A). The Institute of Directors, of which Mr Rogers is an active member, for its part used the opportunity of the review to advocate the abolition of child benefit: 'We believe it to be both economically and socially desirable that families should make the maximum possible direct provision for their children themselves with the exceptions based on those situations which are wholly beyond the control of the family' (*Guardian*, 1 August 1984).

The Institute's concern with state welfare is perhaps understandable, for according to a Low Pay Unit report its own members should be more than able to make direct provision for their children, aided not only by large salaries but by a considerable array of fringe benefits which may include paid holidays, company cars, subsidized housing and pension entitlements. The Low Pay Unit report gave the example of a typical director receiving a salary of £25,000 per year: in addition he would receive a further £12,500 per year in what are somewhat misleadingly called 'fringe benefits', since given their scale they can hardly be conceived of as a marginal reward (Low Pay Unit, 1984). Corporate welfare, however, like the hidden subsidies to the better off afforded by the tax system, most notably on mortgates and occupational pension schemes, were not within the remit of the social security review or indeed of any larger review of government policy.

The social security reviews did signal the government's intention to restructure the benefit system in such a way as to concentrate provision on the 'genuine poor'. Given the government's assertion that the level of welfare spending already constituted a major threat to economic prosperity, the question for the committees was how spending might be better distributed, first to exclude those who were not genuinely poor and secondly to maximize the work incentives of recipients. The questions which were addressed to those who gave evidence to the Review made the new-right assumptions in the Review's agenda explicit. Representatives of particular interest groups were asked from which other groups they thought money should be taken in order to meet any increases which they proposed for their own category of claimants. In a direct pursuit of new-right arguments about the destructive effect of benefit systems on the family, the National Council of One Parent Families was asked about the potential damage to the family structure which could be done by providing single parents with higher benefit levels, thus facilitating marital breakdown.

In a remarkable assertion of the ability of ideology to triumph over common sense, the Supplementary Benefit Review background consultation document made the claim that there had been a continuing rise in the number of those dependent on social assistance 'because of the increases in the real value of the benefit'. In fact, particularly under the Thatcher government, the real value of the benefit had declined. The claim that the increase in the number of people dependent on supplementary benefit could in any sense be connected with an increase in its value made sense only to those who, with their heads buried sufficiently far in monetarist sand, actually believe that people willingly opt for supplementary benefit because of elaborate cost calculations as to how much better off they will be by claiming rather than by taking advantage of imaginary employment opportunities.

The government certainly saw the review as an opportunity to reduce further its commitments in the welfare area, probably by abolishing supplementary benefit entitlement for those under eighteen and replacing it with an allowance, conditional upon participation in education or training, and by abolishing child benefit. Since much of the training would be through YTS, in effect this amounts to the government telling under-eighteens that if they do not take a low-paid placement, often involving menial work for a private employer, they will be denied any benefit.

The attractiveness of the abolition of child benefit which was also mooted lies not only in the considerable savings which would accrue but also in the fact that it would synchronize well with the notion of residual welfare which was at the heart of the Review's intentions. Once the obligations of the state can be confined to those who might be deemed 'absolutely' poor, irrespective of the social nonsense of any such proposition, the way is open for the abolition of a wide range of benefits and the further erosion of the value of those remaining. This in turn would fit in with the larger objective of pricing the poor into work. Denied any form of assistance, increasing numbers of claimants would have little choice but to accept employment in the sweatshop sector of the economy. Although there is little evidence to suggest that benefit levels are so high as to destroy work incentives, it is true that with existing benefit levels family breadwinners are unlikely to work for the kind of wages envisaged by some of the government's supporters. Indeed, as we will see with the privatization of hospital cleaning, these might well amount to no more than £58 per week.

Overall it was estimated that by the middle of 1984 the government had already succeeded, according to rough estimates compiled by the House of Commons library, in cutting £6.5 billion off social security spending. Without the various cuts introduced by the government, social security spending in 1984 would have been £2 billion higher, or the equivalent of more than 2p on income tax (*The Times*, 25 June 1984). In contrast to this treatment of the poor was the government's largesse to upper-income tax payers. In 1984 a total of £4.17 billion was given away as a consequence of income tax changes (over and above indexation) introduced by the Thatcher government since 1979. The top one per cent of tax payers received 44 per cent of this foregone revenue, the bottom 25 per cent a mere three per cent. The average gain for tax units under £5,000 was a mere £20; between £5,000 and £10,000 the gain was £100. In contrast, the average gain for each tax unit between £30,000 and £50,000 was £2,400 and, for those over £50,000, the gain was a massive £11,700 (Roll, 1984, p. 9). When the combined effect of changes in income tax and national insurance contributions was calculated for a married man with two children, those on ten times average earnings were paying 15 per cent less of their income in tax and contributions; those on half average earnings were paying two per cent more (*ibid.*).

5. Health

He'll* privatise forests
Privatise skies
Prisons and schools
He'll bloody privatise.

Privatise the blind
And the dumb and deaf
Privatise the Army
And the RAF.

There's money in cruelty
Money in death
Sell your liver
To buy your next breath.
　　　　　　　　　'Ode to a dying year', Adrian Mitchell

There are powerful reasons we must be ready to consider how far private provision and individual choice can supplement, or in some cases possibly replace, the role of government in health, social security, and education (Howe, 1983)

For many of the new right the existence of a National Health Service is anathema. Health, like most other services and goods, should be provided by a market which will guarantee that services are provided efficiently, in the right amount and in a way which maximizes consumer choice. State provision necessarily leads to inefficiency, to the dominance in the service of the interests of providers rather than the needs of consumers, to inflexibility in the form in which the service is provided, and to a continuing excess of demand over supply. Demand for health care is regarded as infinite when no price mechanism is in operation.

*'He' refers to the year 1984

New rightists dismiss the egalitarian argument that a National Health Service guarantees access to health care for all, irrespective of wealth and income. They argue that some measure of income redistribution, perhaps via a negative income tax, can be directed towards those who are genuinely too poor to take advantage of market remedies and that for most groups the problem of access to health care is not one of money but of consumer choice. Individuals may decide to spend their income on beers and cigarettes or on health insurance for the family. Advocates of privatization recognize that there may be some residual groups who will find it difficult to gain insurance coverage because of age or serious illness and one solution to this problem would be the introduction of full rebates for insurance coverage or a commitment to meeting these medical bills from the public purse (Minford, 1984, p. XI).

Such views are reflected *inter alia* in a Centre for Policy Studies publication which simultaneously captures the apocalyptic vision of the current state of the Health Service and the enthusiastic faith in the virtues of market mechanisms. Thus we find that whilst in 1948 Britain was probably second in the international league of health statistics, 'using the same criteria today we would vie with Italy for bottom place' and 'the gap between our performance and that of comparable nations is widening every year. On the present basis it would cost the equivalent of an additional 25p in the pound on the standard rate of income tax to bridge it' (Jones, 1980, pp. 99 and 100).

Arthur Seldon, a leading new rightist, illustrates the assertive optimism of the marketeers:

> The NHS has done the health of the people a 'dis-service' because it has prevented the development of more spontaneous, organic, local, voluntary and sensitive medical services that would have grown up as incomes rose and medical science and technology advanced. If it were not for the *politically*-controlled NHS we should have seen new forms of medical organization and financing that better reflected *consumer* preferences, requirements and circumstances. (Seldon, 1980, p. 5)

The reiteration of such seemingly self-evident truths is a major element in new-right arguments about the Health Service, and indeed it is rare to encounter any detailed attempt to compare the costs of the Health Service in Britain with those of other western countries, to examine the administrative costs of different models of health care delivery, or to demonstrate empirically the supposed greater consumer satisfaction achieved in private medicine. A leading health expert, Gordon McLachlan, has aptly noted that this belief in the power of the market is 'regarded in many quarters, by no means labelled as collectivist, as an outrageous over-simplification of an approach to a complex of important personal services' (McLachlan, 1982, p. 6).

An occasional political advisor to Margaret Thatcher, David Hart, who, according to a report in the *Daily Mirror*, went bankrupt in 1975 owing nearly £1 million (*Mirror*, 8 December 1983 and 18 October 1984), admirably demonstrates the new-right faith in market panaceas. Writing in the ever-available columns of *The Times* under the headline 'Time to Sell Off the NHS', he asserts:

> Only when the resources that the nation dictates to health care are distributed through a free market will decisions be returned to the consumer, where they belong, and only then will the pound that the individual puts in deliver the maximum care to the patient when it comes out. (Hart, 1983)

Much of the argument against public health care is based on the alleged hijacking of public services by their employees: what June Lait has called 'the coruscating selfishness that appears to inflict some public service employees when compassion goes public' (*Daily Telegraph*, 22 December 1983). Conservative MP Ralph Howell has argued, in an Aims of Industry pamphlet, that the NHS is not only overstaffed by at least 500,000 but that 'in recent years an increasing number of persons, intent on disrupting the service and to use it for political ends, have infiltrated the service and added to the strains' (Howell, 1983, p. 1). Mr Howell does not say where the figure of 500,000 has come from or indeed which categories of employees, and in what proportions, should be dismissed.

Paul Johnson in the *Daily Mail* again captures this obsession with the subversion of the Health Service by its employees:

> The NHS is virtually the only institution in Britain, even in the

public sector, which has continued to expand its staff while reducing its services. Its productivity is appalling, as comparisons with the private health sector show. That is because NHS hospitals are dominated not by doctors and matrons, but by grasping trade unions. (Johnson, 1983)

In contrast to the gross simplification of new-right arguments, problems of inefficiency, cost inflation and unequal access are endemic to health-care systems. A recent international study of experience in Europe, North America and Australia concluded: 'the clear lesson for British policy-makers is that in all these countries both private markets and public activity are inefficient in their use of scarce resources, and hardly effective in meeting whatever distributional goals have been articulated by policy-makers' (McLachlan and Maynard, 1982, p. 532). In contrast to the assumption of a self-regulating market in health, the study concluded: 'it is evident that regulation, the moderation or control of behaviour by the introduction and use of rules, is ubiquitous and inevitable whatever the public/private mix' (*ibid.*).

The common new-right proposition that the NHS is inefficient, overstaffed and burdened with an ever-growing unproductive bureaucracy is certainly not substantiated on any international comparison. In fact the evidence suggests that health services provided by central governments, with budgetary control in government hands, are more susceptible to cost containment, particularly where doctors are paid on a capitation rather than fee-for-service basis. In a survey of a range of EEC countries, Brian Abel-Smith concluded:

Countries which provide an increasing proportion of the population with health care supplied by open-ended insurance and competing providers are much worse placed to control costs. Now the trend is for these countries to try and impose control on the same key elements of supply which successive British governments have controlled for over 30 years. (Abel-Smith, 1979, p. 76.)

The cost of the British Health Service as a proportion of GNP has increased more slowly than that of other countries. In West Germany, for example, expenditure increased from 4.8 per cent of GNP in 1966 to 8 per cent in 1975, and in France from 5.1 per cent in 1966 to 6.8 per cent in 1977 and 8.1 per cent in 1982; in contrast in England and Wales expenditure increased from 4.3 per cent in 1966 to only 5.2 per cent in 1977 and 6 per cent in 1982 (*ibid.*, p. 74; and Abel-Smith, 1984). Significant cost inflation is found in the predominantly private American health-care system, which combines phenomenally high rewards for top medical practitioners with a considerable degree of inequality of access to health-care services. Spending on health care in the United States rose from 6.1 per cent in 1965 to 8.6 per cent in 1975 and 9 per cent in 1979 (Pollitt, 1983, p. 71). In cash terms the United States spends three times as much per head on health care as the UK (Office of Health Economics, 1984). In the United States health-care costs are estimated to be rising at around 12 per cent a year (*Economist*, 1982, p. 28).

There is certainly evidence to suggest the disproportionate growth in administrative and clerical staff in the NHS. Between 1970 and 1980 there was a 48 per cent increase in doctors, a 17 per cent increase in nurses and a 148 per cent increase in administrative and clerical staff (Laurance, 1982A, p. 331). Ironically, many of these new administrators resulted from Sir Keith Joseph's 1974 reorganization of the Health Service. However, between 1975 and 1980, following the introduction of cash limits on health authorities by the Labour government, there is evidence to suggest improvements in hospital efficiency. According to one report, DHSS statistics 'show that all hospital activity (in-patients, out-patients, day cases) increased faster than real costs between 1976 and 1980 . . . In other words, since 1976 at any rate, the NHS has been getting progressively more efficient in terms of the average cost of treating each case' (*ibid.*). Even taking into account the additional administrative burden imposed by Sir Keith Joseph's reforms, the NHS, again in international terms, reveals a remarkable level of cost effectiveness. The proportion of health spending which goes on administration is the lowest of any western country. The administrative costs of the NHS, according to a 1977 OECD report, were 2.6 per cent of total health-care expenditure, compared to 10.8 per cent in France, 10.6 per cent in Belgium, 6.5 per cent in the Netherlands and 5 per cent in Germany (McLachlan and Maynard, 1982, p. 493).

There is in any case good reason to question the equation of growing administrative costs with increasing inefficiency: greater spending on administration might actually increase efficiency. One leading expert has argued that to achieve a greater degree of efficiency in the allocation of health resources a much more effective system of information gathering is required:

> . . . to generate good stocks of information and then to manipulate these stocks in an attempt to monitor the performance of the health care system, public or private, requires considerable resources. Ensuring that health care resources are used efficiently is a resource intensive activity (Maynard, 1983, p. 34).

Health outputs are notoriously difficult to measure, but on one health index based on a composite of health indicators, including premature death and infant and perinatal mortality, Britain comes fourth after Sweden, the Netherlands and Switzerland, while the US is ninth and Germany tenth (Meacher, 1984).

The British system contains great inequalities in access to and utilization of health-care resources but these are considerably less than the grotesque inequalities reflected in the predominantly private American health-care system. A significant number of Americans are not covered by health insurance or by federally funded Medicare and Medicaid programmes, with one estimate suggesting that, in 1982, 50 million Americans were at some point in the year without any coverage (Parker, 1984). Health care remains a major cause of personal bankruptcy in the United States and the dangers faced by the uninsured are sometimes dramatically revealed, as in the case of one uninsured accident victim with serious burns who was refused treatment by forty American hospitals. Only after the Governor of Georgia, the victim's home state, had personally stepped in with a guarantee of a minimum $50,000 contribution to treatment was the patient finally admitted to a hospital. By that time concern was being expressed as to whether he would survive the delays (*Guardian*, 13 May 1982).

Furthermore, those on Medicaid are not always guaranteed treatment. A survey by the Department of Health at Hartford, Connecticut, found that 82 per cent of obstetrician-gynaecologists refused Medicaid patients, presumably because the maximum payment offered by Medicaid was regarded as inadequate (P. Parker, 1984.).

The fact that in reality health-care provision in Britain bore little relationship to the ideological caricature of the new right created some problems for the government.

The government's record: privatizing health

The NHS is safe with us. (Thatcher, 1982)

Soon after the Thatcher government came to office the Royal Commission on the Health Service reported and rejected any change to a system of insurance. The Commission found that the shift to an insurance-based system would not in itself lead to greater resources being devoted to health care and that it would be more expensive administratively. It could also lead to different standards of care being available for those who chose to pay for it, and it would therefore reduce social equity. Secretary of State for the Social Services, Patrick Jenkin, nonetheless established a working party of DHSS officials and specialist advisers to consider further the idea of insurance. In its report this group recommended a more detailed study of ways in which a form of social insurance could be introduced in Britain (Wintour and Wheen, 1982). The new Secretary of State for Social Services, Norman Fowler, showed no enthusiasm for the idea. Even the British Medical Association, previously an enthusiastic advocate of moving to an insurance-based system, began to adopt a more cautious approach, acknowledging in a 1982 paper that an insurance-based system might not provide more funds but could be more expensive to administer (*The Times*, 14 April 1982).

The issue of the future form of funding of the Health Service came to a head in the leaked report of the Central Policy Review Staff in September 1982. This considered a variety of substantive changes in the provision of existing public services. The Report, based on some extremely dubious propositions about the scale and implications of future government spending, explored a variety of alternative ways of financing education and health and welfare services. The Report suggested that £4,000 million a year could be saved by switching to a private insurance scheme in place of the NHS, though for a family of four this would have meant a health insurance bill of £600 per year (*Observer*, 19 September 1982). The hostile reaction which the report engendered from Tory wets and Opposition politicians, coupled with a fear of the electoral consequences of any apparent government threat to the future of these services, produced quick statements of reassurance from a number of Cabinet ministers. Nonetheless it was reported that at this stage the Social Services Secretary, Norman Fowler, was still under pressure from Cabinet hard liners, including Thatcher, to adopt the 'radical option' of replacing the NHS with private health insurance, a strategy which Fowler publicly rejected (*The Times*, 24 September 1982). The study indicated that such a change would *inter alia* mean more bureaucracy and administration and could add massively to the total administrative costs.

In spite of this history the issue of shifting to an insurance-based system was raised again by the new Chancellor, Nigel Lawson. In response, Norman Fowler was compelled publicly to reject the proposal: 'What the advocates of compulsory insurance have to show is that it is ultimately a more effective and efficient way of providing patient care at reasonable cost. I do not believe that that case can be sustained' (*Guardian*, 13 December 1983).

The new right having established the NHS as one of their major targets were, however, unlikely to be moved by the findings of any studies, particularly those conducted by untrustworthy civil servants.

The government not only faced some difficulties in trying to appease its supporters on the right, but it also faced a far more considerable problem in the continued electoral popularity of the National Health Service, a factor which repeatedly forced ministers to make extravagant claims about the government's commitments to, and spending on, health. A 1981 Marplan poll found that more than seven out of ten people thought the NHS was giving value for money. When respondents were asked whether the service should be made private 'with everyone choosing and paying for the service they want' – the logical outcome for the convinced advocate of market solutions – only 13 per cent thought this would be a good thing (*Guardian*, 21 December 1981).

A number of discernible threads in government policy over the first five years can be identified. The government tried to boost the growth of private medicine in a variety of ways; it sought to increase the use of charges for health-care facilities; it sought to privatize areas of the health service and to restrict the growth of the Health Service. This restriction went with a customary statistical sleight of hand as it sought to suggest that, in fact, considerable improvements were taking place.

Private insurance and private medicine

The difficulties of shifting from a tax-based to an insurance-based system nationally did not mean that the growth of private medicine should be curtailed; rather it lent new emphasis to schemes which would allow private medicine to grow, thus reducing demand for NHS services. Dr Gerard Vaughan, Health Minister in the first Thatcher government, envisaged that the private sector would provide around 25 per cent of health care by 1985 (Hencke, 1983). In fact for a number of reasons growth has been much slower than this figure would suggest, though in the early days of the first Thatcher government such projections may not have seemed wildly optimistic. The number of people covered by private health insurance rose by one million between January 1980 and March 1981 (Laurance, 1982B, p. 341). In the two years to 1981 the largest health insurance company, BUPA, increased its membership by 44 per cent and its income by 60 per cent (Laurance, 1983, p. 295). Undoubtedly this growth was helped by the political climate and by fears for the future of the NHS, as well as by concern about the adequacy of current levels of NHS care. Government also gave some more specific assistance. It allowed the costs of private health-care insurance to be offset against tax for those with an income of less than £8,500 per year, a concession which cost the Treasury an estimated £4 million annually (Maynard, 1983, p. 39). And, in the face of protests from the civil service unions, the government early in 1982 offered to negotiate cut-price access to private health-care programmes as part of its civil service pay deal (*Guardian*, 18 February 1982). In spite of union opposition, the government negotiated discounts with BUPA, Private Patients Plan and Western Provident Association (Jones, 1984).

The rapid expansion of health insurance created its own problems, particularly for BUPA. In 1981 BUPA made a loss of £1.9 million and in 1982 the number of subscribers actually fell by 1.2 per cent (Laurance, 1983, p. 295). By 1982 four million people, one in 14 of the population, were covered by private health insurance, as against 1.5 million in 1966, but it appeared that the boom was over. The increasing recruitment of members from social classes three and four placed greater demands on the insurers since, as is well documented, such groups have a lower health status than social classes one and two. In consequence, in 1982 premiums for subscribing companies were raised dramatically, sometimes by 200 per cent. In 1983 and 1984 there were further substantial increases in the cost of subscriptions (*Guardian*, 15 December 1983). The private health insurers faced not only increasing demands from their subscribers but also escalating costs from the providers of services. In the private health insurance market both customers and providers often have an interest in maximizing costs:

> The patient wants the best possible care, and the doctor is there to act as his agent in obtaining it for him. Neither has to pay the bill under an insurance scheme. So it is very easy to pass on cost increases to the insurers, who then load it on to premiums ... Not only is there no incentive for doctors to recommend, or hospital companies to provide, cheaper forms of care, but it makes commercial sense to keep patients in hospital as long as possible. (Laurance, 1983, pp. 295-6)

The private health insurers took a number of measures to try to reduce costs, including seeking to reach agreement with consultants 'for a set level of fees within the scope of benefits'. In seeking such agreement the private health insurers expressed concern that future growth would be difficult as long as the concern over cost escalation remained and that employers would be reluctant to include further groups in schemes 'lest the cost of that benevolence get out of control' (*Guardian*, 1 February 1983). BUPA was forced to indicate that some of its subscribers could be asked to pay for part of their hospital operations if they chose treatment at certain private hospitals which refused to accept BUPA's fee limitations (*Guardian*, 16 December 1982).

The growth of private health insurance was paralleled by the increasing provision of private health-care facilities supported by a number of government measures. The Department of the Environment removed restrictions on the development of private hospitals, which could previously be imposed if there were objections that the NHS would be damaged by the new developments. The Department of Health changed its planning machinery so that no private hospital with fewer than 120 beds required approval from the Secretary of State, while the Department of Industry allowed the Business Start Up Scheme to benefit both private hospitals and a private GP service in North London (Hencke, 1983). Collaboration between the NHS and the private sector was encouraged. In January 1980, NHS consultants, who were not previously allowed to undertake private work, were permitted to earn up to 10 per cent of their NHS income from private patients. This blurring of the distinction between commitment to the NHS and commitment to the private health-care market could only encourage the further development of income-maximizing strategies amongst consultants – strategies which could well involve taking more affluent patients off the waiting list by offering speedier private treatment at the expense of a lengthening waiting list for those whose financial status left them with little choice. The boom in private health insurance had in any case provided a considerable boost to surgeons' incomes. In 1980 the three major private companies paid out a total of £32.67 million in surgeons' fees, a 50 per cent increase on the 1979 figure (L. Fusco, Letters, *Health and Social Services Journal*, 11 March 1982).

The 1980 Health Service Act formally ended the phasing out of pay beds, introduced by the previous Labour government, and gave the Secretary of State power to make NHS services and accommodation available to private patients.

In Glasgow an application to use a new £500,000 brain scanner for private patients provoked protest. The Secretary of the Glasgow Eastern District Local Health Council argued that the approval of the application 'would make an appreciable difference to the waiting list, it would mean private patients would be treated in advance of NHS patients' (*Health and Social Service Journal*, 9 April 1982). It requires no great imagination to appreciate the temptation which such schemes provide to consultants, or indeed to see why such proposals often emanate from the consultants themselves. In effect expensive publicly provided facilities serve to increase the profit to be made from private practice.

The private sector dismissed claims that it was in competition with the public sector for resources or that the private health sector reflected privilege. In the words of Lord Wigoder, Chairman of BUPA:

> I do not want to seem frivolous about a serious issue, but no one in their right mind would survey the beach at Bournemouth, Blackpool and Brighton, observe that there were those who chose to pay for deck chairs, whilst others preferred to lie on the sand, spending their money on ice cream, and then announce that there appears to be two tiers of sunbathers. (*The Times*, letters, 7 October 1982)

It is difficult to believe that the noble Lord really believes that the five million unemployed have chosen to spend their money on ice creams rather than on taking out subscriptions for private health insurance, but perhaps he thinks that the employees of the Pritchard Services Group, the largest supplier of hospital services in the UK and a major beneficiary of the privatization of hospital ancillary services, should negotiate private health-care insurance in their next wages agreement. Since, according to NALGO, the 14,400 employees earn an average of £30 per week, they may encounter some employer resistance (NALGO, 1983).

The proposition that private health care is complementary to rather than in competition with the NHS for resources is equally fatuous. With a finite number of highly trained medical personnel, overwhelmingly trained in the public sector, it is clear that the offer of higher rewards in the private sector will necessarily limit the time such personnel are prepared to devote to the public sector.

In addition, since private medical insurance generally covers a limited range of surgical procedures, resources may be disproportionately directed into such activities at the expense of other population groups with more urgent medical requirements. Those who are insured privately may find it easy to secure an immediate operation for varicose veins; in contrast, those who are not privately insured but who require an urgent operation for a hip replacement may have to wait two years. The existing imbalance between the investment of resources in acute care and in long-term care for the mentally handicapped and the frail elderly will be exacerbated, since the private market makes little contribution in these areas.

The conflict of interest between private medicine and public medicine is frequently self-evident. The resignation of Professor Ian Craft from the Royal Free Hospital in 1981 led to the closure of the only NHS test-tube baby unit. In 1982 the private Cromwell Hospital in London announced the opening of a test-tube baby clinic headed by Professor Craft. The fees for out-patients were announced as £950. For those who wished to stay at the hospital for the three days of the treatment there would be an additional £170 charge per day. It was estimated that patients who were able to pay these fees stood a one in ten chance of becoming pregnant. Compared to the fees charged at Bourn Hall, Cambridge, run by Mr Patrick Stephen and Dr Robert Edwards, it was suggested that those at the Cromwell Hospital were 'cut-price' (*Guardian*, 6 December 1982).

What the advocates of private medicine also ignore is that the existence of a thriving private market removes the sharp elbows of the well healed from the ranks of those demanding a satisfactory public health service.

The growth of the private health-care market and the favourable attitude of the government precipitated a boom in the development of private hospitals. Many of the newcomers into the field were straightforwardly profit-maximizing concerns, in contrast to existing non-profit private-sector groups such as the Nuffield Nursing Homes Trust. In this entrepreneurial climate the major beneficiaries were American health corporations, particularly American Medical International, Hospital Corporation of America, Humana and Community Psychiatric Centres (Wade and Picardie, 1983). When in Glasgow a consortium of 115 Glasgow consultants and American Medical International (Europe) ran into opposition for their plans to open a 102-bed luxury hospital, they were backed by Mr George Younger, Secretary of State for Scotland, who overruled Glasgow District Council's refusal to grant planning permission (*The Times*, 22 October 1982).

Increasing involvement of consultants as direct shareholders in the growth of the corporate health sector was not confined to AMI. Consultants also have a 10 per cent shareholding in three of the Hospital Corporation of America hospitals (Wade and Picardie, 1983). Such involvement not only increases the disparity between the financial situation of consultants in the private sector and the returns available from the NHS, but further blurs the distinction between business ethics and medical ethics.

In an unusual development, precipitated by increasing financial strains within the Health Service, the Tadworth Hospital for chronically ill children was handed over to a consortium of voluntary organizations after the decision of the Great Ormond Street Hospital governors to close it down. The voluntary sector consortium was headed by Timothy Yeo of the Spastics Society, a Conservative candidate soon to be MP for South Suffolk. The government agreed to provide an annual grant to the consortium of private charities which amounted to £890,000 per year for the next three years. The consortium was to provide a further £70,000 per year and it was indicated that local authorities using the hospital might have to pay a fee of around £150 per week (Labour Research Department, 1983, p. 28).

Clearly there is a difference between the universal entitlement to NHS facilities and the qualified entitlement, at the trustees' discretion, to charitable facilities. It was in any case somewhat ironic that the handing over of an NHS facility to the voluntary sector should be widely acclaimed as an innovation. As one commentator noted, one of the reasons behind the formation of the NHS was that voluntary organizations had provided an inadequate framework for the development of the health service (*ibid.*, p. 30)

In the rush of enthusiasm for this new charitable venture the fact that under the new management health workers lost all trade union negotiating rights on pay and conditions scarcely invited comment. Indeed as Mr Yeo, by now an MP, said, the move simply brought the charity into line with other voluntary organizations, which allowed people to join unions but did not allow union negotiations (*Guardian*, 13 March 1984). What Mr Yeo did not add was that this was largely true of those voluntary organizations run by the great and the good to benefit the deserving poor, but then in an atmosphere redolent with Victorian values he perhaps thought this superfluous.

The hospital building boom left the private sector overprovided with beds in some areas, notably in London where, in 1983, it was estimated that some 40 per cent were vacant (Laurance, 1983). The government encouraged the growth of further collaboration with the NHS, and at a fringe meeting of the 1982 Conservative Party Conference, Health Minister Kenneth Clarke suggested that health care subcontractings could be developed:

> There are occasions when the private sector has facilities for a particular treatment in a locality, which the health service cannot satisfy its own demand for. The National Health Service managers can make a choice between capital expenditure on their own account, and contracting out the patient care to a private hospital. (*The Times*, 7 October 1982)

Such a policy would no doubt be extremely advantageous to the private hospitals which already piggyback on the NHS for many of their expensive facilities. Seventy per cent of private hospitals, for example, lack a pathology department and 43 per cent do not have a radiology department. When Margaret Thatcher had an eye operation in a private hospital, essential equipment was borrowed from the NHS (Griffith, 1984). If, in addition, the private hospitals were able to rent out spare capacity to the NHS at private sector prices, the government would have provided them with a filip equivalent to that which it had given to private education through the assisted places scheme.

The cost inflation experienced by the private sector, the increasing expenditure incurred in buying facilities in private hospitals and the overprovision of beds in the private sector contrasts markedly with the bland assurance of one of monetarism's leading apostles, Patrick Minford, that the solution to all problems in the NHS lies in privatization: 'Selling off hospitals, though not politically easy, is a self-contained operation which, once carried out, *guarantees future efficiency*' (Minford, 1984, p. xii; emphasis added).

The mini boom in private medicine did not extend to general practice. A small number of private general practices were set up, but the overwhelming majority of Britain's 27,000 GPs remained in NHS practice. The expansion of private general practice was limited by a number of facts: general practice is not covered by the principal health insurance schemes, there is easier access to NHS GPs than to hospital surgery, and private patients must pay the full cost of their drugs treatment.

In his classic study of the relative merits of different systems of blood donation, Titmuss clearly articulated the dangers of the commercialization of medicine and argued for the benefits of a system which harnessed altruism to the meeting of medical need:

From our study of the private market in blood in the United States we have concluded that the commercialization of blood and donor relationships represses the expression of altruism, erodes the sense of community, lowers scientific standards, limits both personal and professional freedoms, sanctions the making of profits in hospitals and clinical laboratories, legalizes hostility between doctor and patient, subjects critical areas of medicine to the laws of the market place, places immense social costs on those least able to bear them – the poor, the sick and the inept – increases the danger of unethical behaviour in various sectors of medical science and practice, and results in situations in which proportionately more and more blood is supplied by the poor, the unskilled, the unemployed, Negroes and other low income groups and categories of exploited human populations of high blood yielders. Redistribution in terms of blood and blood products from the poor to the rich appears to be one of the dominant effects of the American blood banking system. (Titmuss, 1970, pp. 245-6).

Notwithstanding such strictures, the possibilities for the further penetration of market principles into the delivery of health services seem limitless. A recent letter in the *Lancet*, from Dr Bach of the Harvard Medical School, suggested that the time had come to open up a 'discussion among the medical community' over markets in human kidneys.

There is in fact already a thriving market in imported kidneys, which are brought in from the United States at a cost of more than £1,000 for private transplant operations in Britain (*Guardian*, 10 December 1983). What was novel about this suggestion was the proposal that the market need not be confined to the kidneys of donors who were already dead. Even here, however, it appeared that Dr Bach, far from anticipating developments, was simply reflecting them. It very quickly became known that in Japan a market in live human kidneys was already in operation with prospective donors reportedly being paid up to £8,000. Budding entrepreneurs advertise such services on hospital walls (*Guardian*, 23 November 1984). Bach suggested that there were advantages to be gained from such transactions for both donors and recipients. By selling a kidney the poverty-stricken donor could improve his or her standard of living: 'Should we reject kidney bartering out of hand if the donor could benefit from the exchange, while his kidney may save the recipient's life?' (*Lancet*, 10 November 1984). Bach clearly envisaged the Third World as the primary source of donors, but in principle the arguments could of course be applied to the poor in the west. It no doubt requires only time and the improvement of medical technologies before we might beg'n to talk about markets in other organs, thus completing the circle of exploitation in which the poor are trapped. On the other hand, more than 3,000 kidney patients who die each year in Britain because they are unable to get treatment would receive more immediate benefit from the investment of adequate funds in conventional NHS kidney dyalysis facilities (*The Times*, 16 November 1982).

Refinancing the NHS

In some cases, a system of charging can help to direct resources where they are most required and at the same time induce a sense of priorities among recipients of the services involved. In some cases charges might be a preliminary to some form of private sector involvement. (Sir Geoffrey Howe, 1983)

The development of fee for service provisions is attractive to the new right. Fee for service can be a device for increasingly shifting the cost of provision away from government funding on to the consumer and therefore creating a situation closer to that prevailing in the ordinary marketplace. In the face of political opposition to welfare cutbacks fee increases offer a gradualist alternative to straightforward cuts. The increases also serve as a deterrent to take-up and therefore save money not simply by increasing fee income but also from declining demand. For the free marketeers such a decline in demand reflects no more than the operation of consumer preference in which, given a choice, different individuals will have different preferences relevant to expenditures on dental health or foreign holidays.

The most notable example of increasing fees was in the area of prescriptions. In the first three years of office, the government raised these charges by no less than 650 per cent, from 20 pence in May 1979 to £1.30 in April 1982. The increase in fees not only raised revenue for the Health Service but, by effectively imposing a tax on the sick, it also produced a decline in the number of prescriptions taken out (*The Times*, 3 December 1981). While in general a reduction in the number of drugs consumed should be welcome, there is no reason to suppose that those who failed to take up prescriptions were making rational, health-informed choices. The deterrent effect of the £1.30 charge, which by 1984 had risen to £1.60, would clearly have different implications for the hospital cleaner, employed in the new privatized service, than it would for the director of the expanding multinational.

The deterrent effect of increasing fee levels was also evident in dentistry, where the government substantially increased charges payable by patients. Overall these rose from a maximum of £36 in 1979 to £95 in 1983. A survey conducted for the British Dental Association in 1982-83 found that 18 per cent of women and 11 per cent of men delayed check-ups because of a fear of the likely cost of treatment. Seventeen per cent of lower social classes DE had been put off by cost, against 11 per cent in classes AB (British Dental Association, 1983). For those entitled to assistance in meeting their dental bills the government created further hurdles. The dental means test form *FID* contains some fifty questions and was described by the British Dental Association as representing 'a considerable intellectual hurdle to many patients' (*ibid.*, p. 12).

In a characteristic genuflection to the exigencies of dogma, the government refused the opportunity to save a significant sum of money by cracking down on dental fraud. The revelation that some dentists were receiving up to £150,000 per year from the NHS and NHS patients contributions had increased concern over the possibility of fraud, but a request by the British Dental Association for extra spending of up to £500,000 to monitor dental bills costing £457 million was refused. In a no doubt unintended parody of the government's commitment to *laissez faire*, the Health Minister, Kenneth Clarke, told the BDA that he accepted that some dentists were acting in an unlawful way but said that more dental officers meant fewer staff elsewhere. He suggested that abuse of the existing scheme should not be blamed on the Department of Health (*Guardian*, 22 November 1984). The peculiarity of this conclusion was reinforced by the fact that auditors working for the Comptroller and Auditor General had found that the monitoring of claims made on the NHS by dentists was unsatisfactory and that according to one report 'staff investigating fraud had to spend 80 per cent of their time on other work and lacked computer expertise' (*ibid.*).

One particular category of Health Service users singled out for attention was overseas visitors. Perhaps a victim of its own propaganda, the government clearly believed that there were considerable sums of money to be raised by charging hospital bills to foreign visitors; the charges were intended to raise some £6 million per year (*The Times*, 23 February 1982). Amidst concern about the potential race relations implications of the scheme and considerable doubts about the financial benefits relative to the administrative costs the government went ahead. That such doubts might be firmly based was suggested by the General Secretary of NALGO, who reported:

> In one East Anglian hospital, out of 13,500 forms completed, only five patients were found to be eligible for charges and only one had settled the bill – for the princely sum of £4.50 Estimated costs were £280 for stationery and £450 for staff time. (*Guardian* letters, 27 February 1984)

The use of fees was only one way of increasing the proportion of Health Service costs borne directly by the consumer. Lengthening waiting lists encouraged patients to seek private treatment. Health authorities and hospitals were also encouraged to engage in direct fund raising, inevitably in conflict with other traditionally charitable organizations. At the Normansfield Hospital for mentally handicapped children, for example, a parents' charity provided £22,500 to the Kingston and Richmond Area Health Authority to employ four nursing auxiliaries. It was reported that without the funds the health authority would introduce a partial closure of recreation facilities including a toy library, a hydrotherapy pool and a shop, ironically all provided by parents' fund raising (*Guardian*, 10 December 1981). At the new Milton Keynes hospital a plaque proudly proclaims that even the beds were provided from charitable donations.

Finally, mention should be made of the government's efforts to raise revenue by selling off NHS assets. This included the proposed sale to a private developer of hospital land intended to provide new homes for mentally and physically handicapped people

(*Guardian*, 7 December 1983), and the sale of excess NHS facilities to the private health sector. In a particularly effective demonstration of the government's pursuit of public squalor and private greed it was decided that part of the St. George's Hospital site at Hyde Park Corner, worth millions of pounds, should be sold to Grosvenor Estates for £23,700. The original purchase had included the condition that when the site was no longer to be used for a hospital it should be sold back at the original price to the estate (*The Times*, 25 January 1982). Grosvenor Estates is owned by the Duke of Westminster who inherited it. The Duke is reputedly the richest man in the UK.

Consistent with the government's policy of selling public assets to provide part of its revenue requirements, it was announced, in May 1984, that the government intended to sell off a significant proportion of the residential accommodation for nurses and junior doctors (*Guardian*, 1 April 1984).

Professional monopolies

One of the more intractable problems for advocates of market solutions to the delivery of medical services is the possibility of producer monopolies emerging. These may then limit access to the profession and essentially conspire against the public to maximize the incomes of medical practitioners. The radical solution to this problem is to abolish medical licensure (Friedman, 1962, p. 149). Friedman argues that instead of the dominance of professional associations which exercise an effective monopoly over the right to practice, with consequent restrictions on the quality and variety of medical practice and implications for the cost of medicine, there should be a market in medical services with anyone 'free to practice medicine without restriction except for legal and financial responsibility for any harm done to others through fraud and negligence' (*ibid*., p. 158).

Friedman rejects the argument that special procedures are necessary to guarantee a minimum quality of medicine. Rather:

... the great argument for the market is its tolerance of diversity; its ability to utilize a wide range of special knowledge and capacity. It renders special groups impotent to prevent

experimentation and permits the customers not the producers to decide what will serve the customers best. (*ibid.*,
p. 160)

In fact such is the power of the medical profession that it seems
unlikely that any government of the right, no matter how firmly
committed to monetarist doctrines, would abolish the existing
professional monopoly. Indeed, in the UK the Thatcher government approved a large salary award immediately after coming to
office and continued to approve pay increases for doctors well in
excess of those paid to other Health Service workers. No steps
were taken to increase competition between different branches of
medicine such as, for example, the inclusion of homeopathy within
the NHS, or to encourage more competition in the medical market, for example by allowing dental assistants to carry out a specified range of dental work on their own account.

The one exception to this was the abolition of the restriction on
the sale of glasses to registered opticians. This restriction, introduced in 1958, was abolished in 1984, together with restrictions
on advertising. Opticians did, however, retain their monopoly on
providing prescriptions for glasses. Public concern, reflected in
part through the National Consumer Council and the Consumers
Association, was one factor in the change. It was suggested that
the existing restriction created gross disparities in the pricing
structure and considerable inflation in the retail price of glasses.
The government characteristically also took the opportunity to
abolish the NHS subsidy on lenses and frames except for children
and people on supplementary benefit. As one commentator said
of the bill: 'In other words, it will privatize one corner of the
NHS. This means that about three million customers a year
(40 per cent of the total) will have to pay more for their lenses'
(Laurance, 1984A).

The impoverishment of the poor

The government's unwillingness to challenge the power and privileges of the top medical professionals was not matched by any
similar reluctance to confront low-paid workers in the Health
Service. In the face of public support for the NHS and continuing
pressure from its own back benchers and from groups like the

Centre for Policy Studies, the Adam Smith Institute and the Institute of Economic Affairs for radical changes in the health service, the government concentrated its efforts on seeking to privatize a number of areas of the Health Service. Particular attention was given to activities which were labour intensive, where private contractors would be able to provide much-publicized savings to the NHS by tearing up existing terms and conditions of service. The abolition of the Fair Wages Resolution, which had required private sector employers seeking public sector contracts to observe comparable standards of employment to those pertaining in the public sector, paved the way for such savings.

In pursuing its privatization strategy the government was able simutaneously to appease those of its supporters who declaimed against the slowness of change (not a few of whom had a strong financial stake in the success of privatization) and to achieve so-called efficiency savings. These could be used to justify limits on further central government health spending, whilst privatization implanted within the NHS a Trojan horse. If it could be demonstrated that many of those activities currently carried out within the NHS could be conducted at lower cost by private contractors, clearly the way would be open for the contracting out of further NHS activities. If hospitals could be cleaned by the employees of private firms, if patients could be fed by the employees of private firms, why could hospitals not be managed by private firms or indeed doctors supplied by such firms?

The leak of the contents of a twelve-page confidential draft circular, intended for fourteen regional health authority chairmen in England, in 1983, indicated the direction of government thinking. The document entitled 'Co-operation in the NHS and Private Sector at District Level' suggested that the care of elderly patients could be contracted out to private sector hospitals and that firms could be encouraged to take over the running of wards in NHS hospitals. It suggested that spending £135-£200 per patient per week on accommodation in a private nursing home would be a better alternative to further investment in NHS facilities (*Guardian*, 31 May 1983).

The new right proclaim that privatization, or the contracting out of services currently provided in the public sector to a private company, will almost invariably lead to savings. Michael Forsyth, a former Westminster City Councillor, public relations consultant to Pritchards, one of the largest contract cleaning groups, and a Conservative MP, argues:

> Privatization combines public service with private provision, and represents the attempt to blend public accountability and control of standards with the private enterprise disciplines of efficiency, cost-effectiveness and responsiveness to consumer requirements. As a means of cutting the cost of local government w! ile at the same time improving rather than reducing the services, privatization has been staggeringly successful practically everywhere it has been introduced. (Forsyth, 1981, p. 3)

Subsequent experience did nothing to diminish Forsyth's enthusiasm for privatization. Some controversy occurred when his public relations company, Michael Forsyth Associates, was reportedly responsible for arranging for the Junior Health Minister Mr John Patten to be entertained by firms bidding for NHS contracts. A report from Michael Forsyth Associates claimed that this meeting was instrumental in increasing the pressure on reluctant health districts to put contracts out to tender (*Guardian*, 5 July 1984).

Support for the privatization of ancillary services was not confined to the right of the Conservative Party. The left-of-centre Tory Reform Group (TRG) are also strong supporters of privatization, arguing that the government should move from a position of 'competitive tendering' to one of straight contracting out. In competitive tendering, Health Service employees, already in the NHS, are allowed to compete with private contractors for the work involved. In contracting out, only private contractors are allowed to enter the competition. The TRG argue that under competitive tendering, NHS staff are given an opportunity to frustrate privatization. The TRG share the belief that contracting out is cost effective and further assert that this is not a consequence of reducing wages below the agreed Whitley Council rates:

> Contractors know that if commercial pressures to win business at any cost led to a low wage rate ... The poor performance of low quality staff would damage the whole market. They need to pay higher rates to attract the quality staff needed to clean hospitals. (Tory Reform Group, 1984, p. 41)

Forsyth has actually claimed that staff benefit from privatization: 'They gain a higher status job, more secure in its opportunities for advancement, with higher rates and better benefits and working conditions (Forsyth, 1982, p. 18).

The question of cost effectiveness is not easily resolved, with the claims made on the right for private enterprise being paralleled by claims made on the left for the public sector. For example, one writer recently claimed 'Even health managers now admit that the contracting out of services is more expensive than direct labour' (Oldfield, 1983, p. 90). Both sides are able to provide examples of the relative cost superiority of private or public service provision. In fact much may depend upon such variables as the degree of competitiveness in the contracting process, the willingness of companies to submit loss-leader bids in an attempt to secure a foot in the market, the quality of service provided and, *pace* the TRG, the wage levels of those employed.

It is not necessary to believe in the intrinsic virtue of public enterprise or in the view apparently taken by some left-wing critics that any staff reductions are a negative sign (Whitfield, 1983) to note that a key characteristic of the current privatization move is the substantial erosion of the wages and conditions of service of low-paid Health Service employees. This has been reflected in numerous disputes consequent upon the contracting out of services. The decision by Crothall Hospital Services, a subsidiary of the multinational Pritchard Services Group and a major beneficiary of privatization, to reduce the working hours and thus cut the earnings of their employees at Barking General Hospital in East London byup to 60 per cent, prompted prolonged strike action. Crothall claimed that the cut was necessary to retain the contract against competition from other firms (*Guardian*, 6 June 1984).

The issue of a contract to a private sector employer usually allowed the employer to select which of the existing staff would be taken on. New staff usually faced loss of earnings through a shorter working week and a loss of fringe benefits. Effectively economies were achieved through a combination of declining cleaning standards and a work speed-up process. In order to guard against workforce militancy employers were able to screen out those who were identified as union militants. It was reported that at Barking the only cleaner not offered a new contract was a former NUPE steward, a pattern evidenced elsewhere (Cohen and Anderson, 1984).

Evidence for the Tory Reform Group's claim that cleaning companies would pay 'high rates to attract quality staff' was somewhat sparse. The Cambridge Health Authority contracted out the cleaning of Addenbrooke's Hospital, Cambridge, to Office Cleaning Services (OCS). Cleaning staff walked out in protest against the cuts in pay and conditions which were imposed. The *Guardian* cited the case of one cleaner previously working thirty-four hours per week, including fourteen hours at the weekend for which she received somewhat more than the basic rate, who was also entitled to NHS sick pay, bonus pay, holidays and pension rights. Under the new contract OCS offered to re-employ her for fifteen hours per week with no work at the weekends. Because she was working fewer than nineteen hours per week she would not qualify for statutory sick pay and she would get no pension entitlement. Even the most fervent believer in the private sector's commitment to quality must have been somewhat abashed at the report that OCS had hired children to work on the evening shift, contrary to employment legislation (*Guardian*, 25 October 1984). The government's case was further damaged with the resignation of Professor John Davis, a leading paediatrician, from the Cambridge Health Authority, in protest against political interference in forcing privatization. Professor Davis who professed 'essentially conservative' attitudes argued that the new arrangements militated against the development of caring relations between hospital staff and patients (*ibid.*).

A letter in the *Guardian* eloquently illustrated the tensions between private sector cost cutting, the pursuit of profit-maximizing 'efficiency' and patient care. The writer pointed out that the unnamed company which had employed her not only provided a finite supply of disinfectant, bleach and other equipment for each week, irrespective of whether more was needed, but also had a very narrow view of its employees' role: 'We were explicitly instructed by the management not to talk to the patients in the firm's time. So that, for example, cheering up sick and depressed persons, even for a couple of minutes, was disapprovingly categorized as "wasting time"' (in Labour Research Department, 1982, p. 24).

With increasing competition between cleaning companies to

secure valuable hospital contracts, against a background of high and rising unemployment, it should come as no surprise to apostles of the market that a direct consequence was pressure on the terms and conditions of those employed in the industry. Certainly it was part of the government's intention to use privatization as a means of forcing down wages, as was clear in the abolition of the Fair Wages Resolution. This was followed, in the case of the Ministry of Defence, by a letter to all companies with MOD cleaning contracts, advising them of the change and insisting that all existing contracts with more than six months to run should be reviewed in order to take account of the lower wages which could now be paid (*New Statesman*, 9 December 1983).

When a number of health authorities sought to protect the wages and conditions of ancillary staff in the contracting out process by stipulating holiday entitlement, sickness benefits, pensions and wage rates, Health Minister Kenneth Clarke sought to veto the move. He argued that the authorities' responsibility should be limited to ensuring that only competent contractors tendered and that rates were adequate 'to attract the right sort of staff, given the available supply of full-time or part-time workers in the area' (*Guardian*, 12 October 1984). Given the government's efforts to increase the supply of would-be full- and part-time workers across the country, but more particularly in the North of England, Scotland and Wales, the implication of this for wage levels hardly required spelling out.

The government's interest in cutting the already abysmal wage levels of ancillary staff was further evidenced by the efforts of Mr John Goddard, the principal officer in the DHSS in charge of the privatization programme for hospital cleaning, catering and laundry services. In a series of briefings Mr Goddard is reported to have advised authorities on how to achieve additional savings by further cutting wages, eliminating performance bonds, which provide penalties for companies which fail to fulfill contractual obligations, and charging contractors for fuel. Mr Goddard was reported as saying 'an acceptable contractor need not be a member of the trade association and so should not be required to meet the wage levels recommended by such associations' (*Guardian*, 26 November 1984). This was apparently in response to the efforts made by the Contract Cleaning and Maintenance Association to get its member organizations to tender only at wage levels between £1.72 and £2.10 per hour, the wage levels recommended by the Whitley Council.

That the majesty and resources of government should be deployed to depress the wages of some of the poorest members of society, who had to rely for their defence on an organization of profit-seeking employers, is a vivid illustration of how far Thatcherism had moved the machinery of government away from any concern with social justice or equality.

The government's willingness to let market forces result in deteriorating wages and conditions of employment was evidenced in a major dispute in Medway, where Crothalls lost its eighteen-year-old contract for cleaning four hospitals, in competition with Exclusive Health Care Services, a subsidiary of Brengreen Holdings. Exclusive reportedly intended to replace 157 full-time equivalents with eighty-two full-time equivalents (Paul, 1984, p. 87), and offered to save additional money by not abiding by Whitley Council conditions. When Crothalls appealed to the Health Minister, Kenneth Clarke, he refused to intervene, preferring, according to a report, to allow 'free market forces to dictate pay and conditions' (*Guardian*, 20 October 1984). Observers may have found a note of irony in Crothalls sudden concern for the low paid in that a report earlier in the year had indicated that Crothalls' parent company, Pritchard Services, led the field amongst British companies in South Africa in paying black employees less than the minimum datum level. Some 10 per cent of those 1,400 blacks employed by British firms who were paid less than this level of £128 per month in 1982-83 were employed by Pritchards. Some of Pritchards' female employees were earning only 113 Rand for a forty-six hour week as against the minimum of 223 Rand (*Guardian*, 12 April 1984).

The operation of market forces was further guaranteed by the increasing financial stringency experienced by local health authorities which, faced with a choice of cutting essential services to patients or seeking to make economies in cleaning services, often felt they had no alternative, particularly since central government funding assumed that such 'efficiency savings' would be made.

Contracting out has, to date, been most widespread in hospital cleaning services, but laundry services and catering services are also major targets. In cleaning services existing companies were already poised to move into the field; in laundry services, although requiring more specialist treatment, there were again a number of potential private sector candidates for the work. However, in catering only one hospital contract was held by a private contractor by the end of 1983 (Tory Reform Group, 1984, p. 49). Private caterers' lack of success in breaking into the NHS prompted the advocates of privatization to demand a change in the rules so that instead of a fixed-price system of contracting out there would be a management fee system under which all food, labour and small expenses are charged to the health authority by the contractor and the management fee is levied on top of actual costs (*ibid.*, pp. 50-1).

Conservatives showed a similar concern to ensure that competition between the public and private sector was done on terms most favourable to the latter in the area of hospital laundry and linen-hire contracting. The Tory Reform Group noted that the major advantages of the private sector contract laundries lay in the high levels of capital investment in modern equipment, the ability to run the equipment at full capacity and in lower wage costs. The Group are, not surprisingly, rather coy about this latter point in view of their continual assurances that privatization is not about cutting wage levels below those determined by existing agreements, but they note that the bonus payments in the NHS, which they estimate to be worth 25 per cent of the basic wage, offer one area for economy: 'appointment of a private contractor results in the immediate reduction of these costs' (*ibid.*, p. 66).

The capital equipment advantage of the private sector was of course a function of the government's policy towards the public sector. Indeed it quickly became clear that the intention was to prevent investment in modernizing and improving public sector laundry facilities and, on occasion, to limit the ability of public sector laundries to compete for outside work, hence preventing full utilization of their capacity. Having thus gagged and bound the public sector, ministers were then in a position to push forward their plans for taking advantage of the 'competitive' bids from the private sector.

In 1983 Calderdale Health Authority in West Yorkshire had to abandon improvements to NHS laundry services, and in 1984 Cornwall and Scilly Isles Health Authority were given similar instructions by the government (*Guardian*, 4 January 1984). In both cases the authorities were forced to seek private contractors.

In Newcastle a proposed saving which would have been realized by utilizing the laundry services of the neighbouring Darlington Health Authority was vetoed because it would have breached manpower savings ordered by the Health Minister (*Guardian*, 7 September 1983). It was estimated that Newcastle would have saved £100,000 as against continuing its existing contract with a private laundry. In South Cumbria, ministerial efforts to delay the modernization of the laundry and hence force dependence on private provision resulted in operations being postponed because of a shortage of clean linen (*Guardian*, 5 November 1983). In these conditions it is perhaps not altogether surprising that the private sector has been very successful in winning those contracts which have been put out to tender (Tory Reform Group, 1984, p. 60).

The evidence suggests that ministers will increase their pressure on local health authorities to contract out ancillary services. It is possible that more concessions to private sector lobbyists will be made which will further disadvantage the public sector in competitive tendering. Undoubtedly real savings have been made as a result of contracting out, but many of these have been at the expense of reducing the wages and conditions of service of some of the poorest members of society. The shareholders and directors of the private sector contracting companies have been undoubted beneficiaries, and since these include a number of leading Tories and contributors to Conservative Party funds their influence on government policy has been considerable. Privatization of NHS ancillary services reduces the pressure on NHS spending, appeals to the ideological purists of the new right and lines the pockets of government supporters. Its effect on the users of the health service is less easy to measure; certainly there are good grounds for supposing that the use of private contractors has sometimes resulted in the deterioration of the service provided. A spot check on firms employed by the North-West Thames Authority in 1982 found, according to one report,

> . . . dirty wards, lost records, and an open row between cleaners at an out-patients' clinic . . . A transport firm lost patients' specimens and laboratory reports. Cleaning contractors failed to maintain adequate standards of hygiene in the wards of an inner London hospital. (*Guardian*, 19 February 1983)

Merton and Sutton Health Authority, a Conservative-controlled group, voted to keep domestic services at its hospitals under direct labour after investigating the standards of some of those private companies which were contracting for the job. It was suggested that the existing standards of work these companies were providing, under other health contracts with similar authorities, together with the specifications provided in their tenders, did not guarantee an adequate standard of service (*Tribune*, 27 January 1984).

Jane Paul has drawn attention to the risks involved to health service users in privatization:

> If standards fall in ancillary work, the health service becomes unhealthy. When costs are cut in labour-intensive services, standards are bound to fall. Corners are cut to get the job done in less time with fewer staff. Cleaning will be less thorough and less frequent. Laundry will be less carefully checked and sorted, risking contamination of 'clean' linen from other sources. Training will be minimal and less effectively monitored. Supplies will run short or may be rationed. Nutritional standards will fall. In every case, the service will be less flexible and less responsive to the immediate needs of the authority, the patients and the other medical staff. The real danger is that hygiene and safety standards will drop – resulting in more cross-infection, wound infections and post-operative problems, with more accidents to patients, staff and equipment and there will be increased public risks if serious diseases or dangerous pathogens are inadvertently spread to the community outside. (Paul, 1984, p. 91)

Professional power and monopoly profits

The government's enthusiasm for pursuing measures which would save Health Service money at the expense of low-paid employees was not paralleled by any similar commitment to save Health Service monies at the expense of the excessive profits of those businesses supplying drugs and other commodities to the Health Service. In pursuing policies which left the DHSS as the patron of companies extracting disproportionately large profits from the sale to the public sector of goods with not altogether benign consequences the government was doing no more than continue the policy of previous governments, both Labour and Conservative. Indeed the relationship between the DHSS and private sector companies supplying medical goods is as clear an indication as could be found of a lack of concern with cost effectiveness in the public sector.

The pharmaceutical industry has relied on the system of licensing new and existing products to protect monopoly profits. Such products are frequently no different in their effect and sometimes less beneficial than existing generic drugs available at a fraction of the price. The excessive profits which the pharmaceutical industry earn are then used, in part, to foster a relationship with medical practitioners in which medical ethics are quickly replaced by mutual avarice. Most of the major medical magazines depend for their existence on drug advertising which thus permeates not simply their advertising columns but also their editorial policy. General practitioners will be visited regularly by representatives of the drug companies to be wined, dined and presented with everything from golf clubs to office clocks. New surgeries may rely on the drug companies for the lavish provision of free wine and food for the opening occasion. Doctors will be entertained not simply in expensive local restaurants but, on a big promotion, perhaps aboard a luxury yacht. One letter to Merseyside doctors from a large Italian drug company promoting a new drug to help arthritis sufferers urged doctors to attend the presentation and buffet aboard Henry Ford's motor yacht, to sample

> an era that has almost vanished from our consciousness. When you tread the thick carpets, sit in the deep arm chairs, and examine the elaborate chandeliers and heavy wood panelling you will find yourself back in that protective period between two world wars when, for some people at least, time passed agreeably enough. (*Guardian*, 15 January 1983).

Such inducements are not confined to general practitioners. Senior hospital medical staff are a prime target, and on another occasion a group of rheumatologists considered the benefits of another new drug on an all-expenses-paid trip to Venice aboard the Orient Express (*Guardian*, 2 February 1983). For those doctors for whom this array of untaxed fringe benefits was an insufficient reward for their close partnership with the drugs industry, there was also the opportunity to engage in tests of new drugs, with unproven safety records, on unwitting patients in return for an appropriate financial reward. This could be arranged through the Medicines Surveillance Organization Ltd., a wholly owned subsidiary of the Royal College of General Practitioners. According to reports, one drug, Suprol, which was tested in this fashion, could have serious side effects and might be given to patients who would otherwise receive an established mild painkiller (*Guardian*, 13 November 1984). Doctors were paid a reported £36 for engaging in this test, but the growing controversy over the ethics of commercial incentives led to moves to terminate such tests (*Guardian*, 28 November 1984).

The power and influence of the drug companies had a number of negative consequences, most importantly in encouraging the overprescription of drugs. Medical intervention is frequently synonymous with drug prescriptions. Powerful interests which back the ever-expanding role of drugs are absent when it comes to the development of holistic approaches to medicine. One consequence of overprescription is the increasing incidence of drug-induced disease and premature death from the side effects of drugs. The scale of the problem is suggested in the field of tranquillizers where patients, frequently suffering stresses created within the wider society, have their problems dealt with by drug prescription. In 1980 about 14 per cent of the adult British population took minor tranquillizers at some time, with 1.5 per cent having been on them for more than a year (*New Society*, 23 February 1984). One American expert, Professor Karon, has suggested that 'drugs are causing as much mental illness as they cure. And because of the money manufacturers spend on research, psychotherapy is having even less influence on mental policy, despite our findings' (Berry, 1984). A second consequence of existing prescription policies lies in the excessive cost to the Health Service caused by unnecessary prescribing and the prescribing of expensive brand-named drugs rather than cheaper generic substitutes.

The essential question faced by the government was whether it would accept the recommendation of the Greenfield Committee that chemists should be allowed to substitute unbranded generic drugs for more expensive brand-named equivalents. In taking such a step the government would not only have had to intervene in the marketplace, contrary to its well-known aversion to such intervention, but it would also have had to challenge the prerogatives of the medical profession. Given the rewarding links between the medical profession and the drug companies, it is not altogether surprising that the BMA generally opposes any limitation on doctors' rights to prescribe whatever drug they wish.

The ideological reluctance of the Conservatives to engage in such intervention, together with their natural disinclination to offend powerful corporate and professional interest groups, made the outcome easily predictable. The government rejected the Greenfield Committee's recommendation and engaged instead in a series of cosmetic manoeuvres intended to suggest that significant savings would be made in the nation's drug bill but which would not have much real effect on drug company profits.

In 1983 the Committee of Public Accounts of the House of Commons reported that nine drug companies alone had made £33 million in excess profits from the NHS over a two-year period. The Committee expressed concern that the DHSS allowed drug companies to make profits of 25 per cent on capital as against the 22 per cent allowed in defence contracts, and the average, which the Committee thought reasonable, which would have been a rate of 17 per cent. This rate was certainly not ungenerous since according to the CBI the average pre-tax rate of return on capital for industrial and commercial companies ranged between 6.8 per cent and eight per cent from 1980 to 1982. In fact three or four of the largest drug companies had made profits of up to 35 per cent. The Committee also noted that as a consequence of various corporate financial manoeuvres – notably transfer pricing in which firms buy from foreign parent companies at inflated prices – the top sixty drug companies, which made profits of £252 million from the NHS in 1979-80, paid only £36 million in corporation tax, which should be levied at 52 per cent of profits (*Guardian*, 26 May 1983).

The government's response to these excessive profits came with the Social Services Secretary Norman Fowler's declaration that he would save £25 million on the drugs bill in the next year. The amount to be saved accounted for no more than 1.25 per cent of the NHS drugs bill (*Guardian*, 25 July 1983). In December

1984 the amount of profit firms were allowed to make on capital was cut from 25 per cent to 21 per cent. In view of the inability of the DHSS to control the real levels of profit which were being made, the government's ability to achieve real cuts could reasonably merit some scepticism. In fact, as the *Guardian* correspondent Andrew Veitch reported, although there was a short-term reduction in prices they quickly started to rise again (*Guardian*, 18 July 1984).

In the meantime the Association of the British Pharmaceutical Industry was able to announce that its new president would be Dr John Griffin, whose previous appointment had been with the DHSS, where his job was to control the safety of drugs and the way that drug companies promoted their goods to the medical profession. This unusually swift move from policing the drugs industry to promoting it was approved by the DHSS and by the Advisory Committee which considers whether it is proper for senior civil servants to take jobs in related industries (*Guardian*, 21 July 1984).

In November 1984, under continuing public and political pressure, the Social Services Secretary announced that in future the Ministry would refuse to pay for a number of specified branded drugs which could be replaced by cheaper generic substitutes. It is too early to know whether this will have any significant effect on the national drugs bill or on the industries' profits, but the move produced a predictable protest from the British Medical Association. The announcement the previous month that, following the price freeze introduced in 1983, drug prices had actually risen by 10 per cent gave little reason to suppose that these latest measures would have much effect (*Guardian*, 2 October 1984). Characteristically the government used the smokescreen created by the furore over its limitation of the freedom of GPs to prescribe by removing a number of medicines from the approved list, such as the cough medicine Actifed, which it was felt patients should pay for over the counter. The effect of this change is to increase the health costs of low-income groups who are entitled to free prescriptions. A further implication of the proposed charge is that an increasing number of medicines could be removed from the NHS but remain available for those willing to pay privately. This could be done irrespective of whether a genuinely generic substitute remained available to NHS patients.

One remedy which should in principle have been attractive to a government committed to the operation of market forces would have been the abolition of restrictions on 'parallel importing'. This would have enabled a number of drugs to be purchased abroad at prices well below those obtaining in the British market. A *Times* report cited, for example, Beecham's Amoxil antibiotics which cost the NHS £81.50 for 500, available in Singapore for £35, and Wellcome's Zyloric arthritis tablets available to the NHS at £14.34 for 100 but obtainable overseas at £3.00 (*The Times*, 3 July 1982). Such a move would of course have had a deleterious effect on drug company profits. Claims that parallel importing could endanger health because of the absence of quality controls failed to deal with the fact that a market in such drugs reportedly already exists and that restrictions cover areas including other EEC countries which maintain high standards of quality control.

The government's protective attitude towards the drugs industry also encompassed an unwillingness to take action against misleading drug advertisements. One expert, J. Collier, described the placing of such adverts as 'commonplace', and in a letter to the *Lancet* cited a number of cases in which he claimed that clearly misleading claims were made for particular drugs (Collier, 1984).

Firms which engage in misleading advertising to doctors are liable to prosecution, but although the Health Minister Kenneth Clarke acknowledged that even his officials had identified thirty-one breaches over a one-year period, no firm had been prosecuted (*Guardian*, 30 November 1984). It was perhaps unfortunate that the government's wider concern with law and order should be absent in an area where such misrepresentation not only leads to excessive public expenditure by promoting the dubious benefits of expensive brand-named drugs, but also endangers patient life and health. No doubt consistent with their wider philosophy, the government was relying on the self-policing of the pharmaceutical industry which maintains its own Code of Practice Committee to ensure compliance with the industry's code. However, the frequency and degree of misrepresentation contained in adverts suggests that the use of the 'sleeping policeman' is not confined to traffic management.

The contrast between the vigorous pursuit of market forces in the privatization of health services and the protected environment which the DHSS created for the pharmaceutical industry could scarcely be more marked. Low-paid hospital workers could see their terms and conditions of service torn up overnight, irrespective of growing evidence that privatization threatened the maintenance of standards of hygiene and patient care (TUC, 1984); drug companies, in contrast, could rely on support from Conservative backbenchers all the way up to the Prime Minister, who personally vetoed a proposal that the DHSS should cease to have as one of its obligations the fostering of the pharmaceutical industry (*Guardian*, 10 November 1984).

The common link which connects the government's apparently contradictory attitudes is its concern to protect and enhance the profitability of the private sector. This could be done by opening up new areas for corporate enterprise, as in the privatization of ancillary services; in contrast, any action on prescription patterns and drug company pricing would necessarily reduce the very high levels of profit enjoyed by the drugs industry. It is perhaps not surprising that a number of commentators share the view of the late, distinguished Keynesian economist, Joan Robinson, who suggested that monetarism is but a fig leaf behind which the rich pursue their class interests (Open University, 1982).

Conclusion

The question of the level of government spending on health was a subject of continuing controversy for the Thatcher government. For its part the government claimed that expenditure was in fact increasing, in real terms, whilst the Opposition continued to draw attention to cuts in provision. In fact both sides could claim some evidence for their case, but the flaw in the government's argument was that although expenditure increased in real terms it failed to keep pace with increasing demand or to take adequate account of the particular kinds of cost inflation experienced in the health-care system. In the five-year period from 1973-74 to 1978-79, most of which was covered by Labour governments, health spending increased by 18.6 per cent in real terms and, in the following five years, by 15.1 per cent (Meacher, 1984). However, an increase of nearly 10 per cent beyond the level of the Retail Price Index was required simply to compensate for the higher level of inflation experienced within the Health Service.

The major demographic factor affecting the Health Service was the increasing number of elderly in the population. It has been calculated that a person aged between sixty-five and seventy-four costs the hospital and community health services four times as much as a person aged between sixteen and sixty-four, and that for a person over the age of seventy-five the cost is nine times as great (*Guardian*, 1 June 1984). The greater cost inflation experienced in the Health Service is in part accounted for by scientific and technological advances which enable patient life to be prolonged but often at the expense of intensive high-cost surgery and aftercare. The prestige of the high-technology specialisms and the power they wield in the hospital hierarchy ensures that resources are diverted into these areas at the expense of less influential specialisms.

The resource pressures on hospitals were aggravated by the fact that a disproportionate amount of the total health increase went on GP services, in part to finance the large pay rises awarded to the medical practitioners soon after the Thatcher government's election. Hospitals were further constrained by the staffing cuts imposed on district health authorities and by the need for higher-spending authorities to achieve greater economies as part of a continuing programme to achieve a greater geographic equality in the distribution of Health Service resources. The overall effect was an increase in hospital waiting lists which had grown to 700,000 by 1984, including some 200,000 who had waited for more than a year (*Guardian*, 10 October 1984).

The dramatic proposals of the Oxford Regional Health Authority, which included asking patients to provide their own food, pay for non-urgent surgery and family planning services, pay for their own accommodation while being treated and fulfill a residential requirement in order to qualify for health care, have not to date been implemented. A survey by the *Guardian* in early 1984 did however find a pattern of cuts, ward closures and job losses across health authorities and 'a disturbing trend of authorities economising by postponing improvements promised for the elderly, mentally ill, and handicapped' (*Guardian*, 18 January 1984). The effect of cuts and inadequate financing was seen not simply in growing waiting lists and the neglect of the cinderella areas of medicine, it was also in the premature death and unnecessary disablement of those affected. A survey of the treatment of premature babies needing intensive care in the South East of England found that a third failed to receive the specialist attention needed because there were not enough cots or nurses to treat them. Instead they were sent to district hospitals where it was reported they were more likely to die or to survive but be handicapped because of a lack of specialist equipment (*Guardian*, 29 November 1982).

The dilemma the government faced in the Health Service was that this was obviously an area targetted for cutbacks in public sector spending yet it remained an area of acute electoral sensitivity. The indications are that the Thatcherite strategy will continue to be to seek areas for privatization, to obscure the actual situation by meaningless statistical flourishes which serve to create the illusion that in some real sense health services are being improved, whilst further tightening control over the growth in the Health Service budget. In 1984 it was indicated that NHS spending would grow by one per cent in real terms, as measured by the Retail Price Index; in practice, because the Retail Price Index significantly underestimates the actual increase in costs beyond the inflation rate experienced by the Health Service and because of the demographic factors already mentioned, this meant a further cut in services provided.

The government continued to pursue the goal of greater business efficiency in the NHS with the appointment of a new class of super-managers, wherever possible recruited from the private sector. The first Managing Director to the National Health Service was appointed at a salary of £70,000 per year, then almost twice the civil service salary for the equivalent rank. The man appointed, Victor Paige, Chairman of the Port of London Authority and Deputy Chairman of the National Freight Consortium, made a somewhat inauspicious start to the job when he told his first press conference that not only did he have private health insurance but 'most people have it nowadays' (*Guardian*, 14 December 1984). It was perhaps a curiously British demonstration of business efficiency to display such a lack of familiarity with the product market.

Faced with the perceived need to cut Health Service spending the government could have sought measures to reduce the demand on health services, notably by promoting health education and by tackling some of the known causes of disease. To do so, however, would have contradicted the government's broader *laissez faire* philosophy. The government refused to take any action to restrict cigarette advertising further, or to prevent back-door advertising through sports sponsorship, in spite of evidence that tough legislative approaches could substantially reduce tobacco consumption (Findings, *New Society*, 8 November 1984). The government's attitude towards broader health education issues was illustrated by its attempt to suppress the report of the National Advisory Committee for Nutrition Education and by its encouragement to the Health Education Council to strengthen its industrial links, including seeking sponsorship from the alcohol and soft drinks industries (*Guardian*, 6 December 1983). The appointment to the Council of the anti-smoking campaigner Michael Daube was allegedly blocked on the grounds that he would be unacceptable to ministers.

Faced with mounting evidence of disease and premature death from increased alcohol consumption, as the relative cost of alcohol declined, the government unhesitatingly suggested that the problem was one for individual doctors to tackle. To expressions of widespread disbelief, the Junior Health Minister, John Patten, told a British Medical Association Conference on alcoholism: 'we would like you to tackle the problem urgently because there is no way we can tackle the problems centrally' (*Guardian*, 29 November 1984). This demonstration of fealty to the fundamentals of Thatcherite non-interventionism was completely at variance with the views of leading experts who believed that the key lay in increasing taxation and a greater emphasis on health education, both of which require government action.

Finally, in a demonstration of the government's endless pursuit of private alternatives, ministers suggested that in future the Department of Health's advertising campaign to deter excessive drinking by drivers at Christmas should be taken over by the private sector. A suitable sponsor, it was suggested, would be the drinks industry (BBC, Jimmy Young Programme, 7 December 1984).

6. The Personal Social Services

We hear a lot today about social work, perhaps the most important social work is motherhood. (Patrick Jenkin, Secretaty of State for Social Services, 1979-81, Speech to the 1977 Conservative Party Conference)

Putting markets and competition to work in the nation's interests is not just a policy for industry or local government. It is an approach which has as yet barely impinged upon the apparatus of the welfare state . . . In some cases, a system of charging can help to direct resources where they are most required and at the same time induce a sense of priority among recipients of the services involved. In some cases charges might be a preliminary to some form of private sector involvement. (Sir Geoffrey Howe, 1983)

The government's strategy towards the personal social services was reflected in a number of linked themes: the need to contain, and if possible curtail, expenditure; the desire to shift both the expectation and the reality of service provision away from the statutory authorities and on to the family, the community and the voluntary sector, and the search for areas which offered potential for privatization.

In response to the economic recession, which followed its early forays into monetarism, the government sought to achieve considerable cutbacks in local authority spending on personal social services. Government expenditure forecasts indicated a cut of 6.7 per cent in real terms for 1980-81 but local authorities used their relative autonomy from central control to afford a measure of special protection to the personal social services and held spending at pre-existing levels (Webb and Wistow, 1982A).

This did not prevent a decline in the levels of provision. Local authorities were, in general, unable to raise the level of expenditure in line with increases in costs or to allocate additional resources to meet increases in demand, precipitated by demographic changes and the adverse social consequences of government economic policy, which generated increasing demand from social service clients.

The special protection afforded to the personal social services will not survive increasing government pressure on local authority finances, most recently through the introduction of rate-capping. The direct consequence of this will be a further decline in levels of service provision. In 1983-84 local authorities budgetted for an expenditure of £2,163 million on social services, seven per cent above the expenditure level laid down in the Rate Support Grant Order (Stewart, 1984). In some authorities the level of 'overspending' is immense. Amongst the thirty-three London boroughs, only two or three were not spending above the government limit for 1983-84. Camden was overspending to the tune of 44 per cent of its social service budget. In Harringey the overspending on social services was calculated to be £6.5 million on a £23 million annual budget (Townsend, 1984). Given the scale of the perceived overspending, and the government's intention of reclaiming such overspending, local authorities will no longer have the freedom to protect the personal social services. Indeed it seems probable, given the cumulative nature of central government pressures, that personal social service spending will have to be severely reduced. For example, a survey by the Local Government Campaign Unit of sixty-two authorities spending more than £10 million per year, and which were above government guidelines, found that nearly all would have to cut spending on nursery schools, day nurseries and grants for voluntary organizations providing care to the under-fives (Penn and Simpson, 1984).

Cutbacks occur not against the background of resource extravagance but often in a context of acute pressure. A study commissioned by the Department of Health and Social Security, published in 1982, found that understaffing and inexperience amongst social service departments and social workers caring for children at risk were major factors in a number of serious cases of child abuse (DHSS, 1982). Another research project found that one in ten children taken into care would have to stay with ten or more foster parents or children's homes (*Guardian*, 29 September 1982). An inquiry into the death of Shirley Woodcock, taken into care by Hammersmith Social Services Department, described the Department's policy as 'fostering at all costs' and noted that one factor in the council's failure to provide adequate care was staffing levels: 'It has to be stated categorically that the staffing levels within the area teams of both social work and administrative personnel are such that any absence . . . cannot be covered adequately by remaining staff.' The inquiry suggested that if the council was unable to carry out its statutory duties then the Social Services Policy Committee should 'issue a clear statement of priorities, which acknowledges that, given present resources, some services cannot be provided' (*Community Care*, 20 January 1983). This paralleled the finding of the chairman of a panel of inquiry into the earlier death of Lucy Gates, who had been left by Bexley Social Services Department in the care of her mother. Mr Arthur Mildon, QC, Chairman of the Panel of Inquiry into her death in a fire which occurred while her mother was out, concluded: 'If in the present economic climate more money cannot be made available for supporting families at risk in their own homes, then, if their children are to be safeguarded more may have to be separated from their parents with the financial and social consequences which the alternative course will entail' (*Guardian*, 13 November 1982).

Faced with a growing disparity between the provision of social services and the need for them, local authorities, particularly those of a Thatcherite hue, sought to increase the use of charges for services. Such charges not only increased council income but could also serve as a major deterrent to take-up. The introduction of charges for home-helps for elderly and disabled people by Redbridge Borough Council resulted in 286 people cancelling their home-help service, of whom 236 were old or disabled people dependent on supplementary benefit or with gross incomes below £35 per week (*Sunday Times*, 14 September 1980). Most social workers were unenthusiastic about charges but the Director of Croydon Social Services, Nigel Grindod, saw some scope for raising revenue by charging for social work services: 'The idea came to me when we were asked by the Council to look at ways of raising money. After all, you have to pay to go and see the dentist or have your eyes tested, so why not when you see a social worker?' (*Guardian*, 28 October 1981).

Increasing the use of fees was not the only way of producing additional revenue. Cambridgeshire County Council, in the face of protests from the voluntary sector and enthusiasm from government ministers, announced that it intended to launch a charity appeal for its social services department and voluntary groups. The council indicated that it intended to appoint a private fund-raising agency at a fee of close to £10,000 to raise £50,000 from industry (*Guardian*, 18 November 1982).

Clearly if government spending on welfare services was to be reduced and local authority spending on the personal social services was to be severely limited, some other provision would need to be made for those who would otherwise be social service clients. The government's answer to this problem was to be found in the development of community care. In practice, emphasis was increasingly to be placed on the responsibility of the family and the community for making service provision. Social workers were to be enablers in a larger caring network which increasingly sought to involve volunteers within the community and to mobilize family resources. This strategy was also abetted by the increasing use of special schemes which sought to recruit the unemployed for voluntary work, notably through the Community Programme. Through such schemes the government was able simultaneously to massage the unemployment statistics and bring in low-paid workers to perform social service tasks.

The redirection of expectations and service provision away from central and local government and on to the family, the community and the voluntary sector constituted a plausible redirection of activity consistent with the new right's broader view of the appropriate role of the public sector. In practice, however, it resulted in a situation where, for many people, care was not provided in the community or by social services, whilst families found themselves not so much encouraged to participate in informal caring networks as compelled to provide care in the absence of any alternatives.

Community care

I don't think that mothers have the same right to work as fathers. If the good Lord had intended us to have equal rights to go out to work, he wouldn't have created man and woman.

(Patrick Jenkin, 1979, Secretary of State for Social Services)

We must put the responsibility for day-to-day help back where it firmly belongs, into the communities in which elderly people live. (Patrick Jenkin, 1980)

The alternative to the institution has been to be herded into newly emerging 'deviant ghettoes', sewers of human misery and what is conventionally defined as social pathology, within which (largely hidden from outside inspection or even noticed) society's refuse may be repressively tolerated. Many become lost in the interstices of social life, and turn into drifting inhabitants of those traditional resorts of the down and out, Salvation Army hostels, settlement houses and so on. Others are grist for new, privately run, profit-oriented mills for the disposal of the unwanted – old-age homes, half-way houses and the like. (Scull, 1977, p. 153)

A man who lived in a dog kennel turned to petty crime to try to be sent back to a mental hospital where he had spent 20 years, a psychiatrist told Teeside Crown Court yesterday. But no state hospital could find a place. (*Guardian*, 30 June 1982)

One result of the increasing resource constraints in social services was the considerable difficulty in implementing the intended shift of provision for certain client groups away from the NHS and on to community-based personal social services. Community care was seen as being a more desirable and cost effective means of dealing with the needs of a significant proportion of the elderly and those experiencing a range of disabilities. A successful shift to community care would have required a considerable increase in central government funding for community-care facilities and services. In the London borough of Wandsworth, frequently seen as a Thatcherite showpiece, cuts included the closure of a day centre for the mentally ill and the reversal of a proposal to use an unneeded children's home for mentally handicapped children who would otherwise be dependent on long-stay hospitals (*Guardian*, 21 January 1981).

One expert appraisal of the effect of the failure to raise spending on local authority social services in line with increased costs and growing demand concluded:

The result has been reduced service cover for the elderly . . . if real reductions on spending on personal social services were now to take place . . . the ability of local authorities to support caring families and community networks would be further undermined. Community care could increasingly come to mean 'abandoned in the community'. (Webb and Wistow, 1982B)

The accuracy of this prediction was soon evident. In 1984 the Spastics Society announced that it planned to close waiting lists for residential care because it was no longer able to deal with the volume of applications from people seeking an escape from inadequate provisions for handicapped people living in the community. The society claimed that the problem had arisen because the government had increased its programme of moving the mentally-ill and handicapped out of hospitals and into the community whilst social service departments did not have the resources to cope. It cited as evidence of those affected the case of a severely disabled fifty-three-year-old without any schooling who was now being looked after by her eighty-three-year-old arthritic mother and a forty-one-year-old woman, who had been in a hospital for the mentally handicapped for twenty-nine years and now had to be trained to look after herself (*Guardian*, 15 April 1984).

In the United States, where the move to deinstitutionalization and 'community care' is well established, the consequences of inadequate resourcing are already apparent:

Today there are estimated to be at least 36,000 sober but unwashed men and women who inhabit the streets of virtually every New York neighbourhood, sleeping in subways, eating out of garbage cans. Some are former inmates of New York mental institutions, which, for financial reasons, have been releasing their harmless cases without too much enquiry as to who else could care for them. Others are refugees from 'welfare hostels' where an overwhelmed Department of Social Services has been housing the city's indigent – dreadful, rat-infested tenements where the poor prey on the poor. (Egginton, 1981)

Clearly the scale of the problem in Britain has not yet reached

American proportions, but one study of 100 patients discharged from a large mental hospital revealed the consequences of grotesquely inadequate care facilities in the community. It found that many of those discharged 'suffered extreme loneliness and isolation'. Twenty-six of the ex-patients had children under eighteen and sixteen of these 'complained of severe difficulties in child management, ranging from aggressiveness and temper tantrums to bed wetting after seven years, and failure to thrive ... Over half these families had no contact with the social services at all.' For some of those discharged, the absence of adequate care facilities had fatal consequences: 'By the time the study was in its sixth month, four patients had killed themselves' (Quine, 1981).

More widely publicized in the UK has been the increasing burden placed upon carers as a consequence of cutbacks in institutional provision and community support. Predominantly, as Finch and Groves have argued, the burden falls on women:

> An examination of community care, in a situation where there is minimal input of statutory resources, reveals that the provision of primary caring falls not upon 'the community' but upon identifiable groups and individuals, in a way which is not necessarily equitable. Indeed, this can be best expressed in terms of a double equation – that in practice community care equals care by the family, and in practice care by the family equals care by women. (Finch and Groves, 1980, p. 494)

This argument is supported by the findings of a Policy Studies Institute Report (Nissel and Bonnerjea, 1982) on the care of the elderly, which found that when elderly parents moved in women were compelled to cease work whilst receiving little help in caring from either children or husbands. In spite of mounting evidence of the deleterious consequences for women, the government nonetheless refused to extend the Invalid Care Allowance to married women, for whom caring was presumed to be a function of their marital duties (Bowling, 1984).

The introduction by the Health Service, in 1984, of the Hospital at Home scheme, will place a further burden on carers in the family. Indeed in the light of the government's record in putting resources into community-care programmes, the Hospital at Home scheme is a 'sick joke' since in effect it legitimizes leaving people who suffer strokes or other sudden collapses in their own homes. There they may be visited by a community nurse, but the major burden of care will fall on the family, and hence on the woman who will be expected to give up work to provide the necessary care.

Community-care strategies have been inadequate not only in their failure to provide an adequate array of aids to independent living, whether through the support of social services staff or the provision of necessary special equipment, but also at a more basic level. Every year a large number of old people are at risk from hypothermia. The precise number of deaths caused by hypothermia is unknown. Government estimates based on death certificate figures seek to place the number around one or two dozen per year. Independent estimates would rank the figure much higher than this. One survey of over 1,000 old people found that 54 per cent had living-room temperatures below 60.8°F, the minimum temperature specified in the Offices, Shops and Railway Premises Act of 1963 (Wicks, 1982). Some 10 per cent of those surveyed had deep body temperatures just above the hypothermic level. The survey was conducted in 1972, at which time the DHSS had issued an advisory leaflet *Keeping Warm in Winter* which urged old people to keep their living-room temperatures at about 70°F. Some years later this recommendation was quietly withdrawn, a move defended by DHSS Minister Linda Chalker in December 1979 when she told the Cold Conditions Conference that the recommended temperature was an interference with individual freedom and conjured up a vision of *1984* (Wicks, 1980). It is of course more fully in keeping with the Orwellian spirit of *1984* that politicians' rhetorical flourishes should obscure the fact that for many of the elderly the freedom concerned is the freedom to freeze.

The great and the good

I am very encouraged by the way in which local authorities, Directors of Social Services, the social work profession and the specialist press are increasingly determined to shift the emphasis of statutory provision so that it becomes an enabling service, a statutory provision enabling the volunteers to do their job more effectively. (Margaret Thatcher, 1981)

Privatization does not have to take place through commercial organizations. It can equally well be effected by the use of voluntary organizations. (Tim Yeo, MP, former Director of the Spastics Society, 1984)

Care in – rather than out of – the community has received increased emphasis in recent years. Not so much because of resource constraints – though resource constraints there have undoubtedly been. But rather the human and social advantages of caring for the elderly in their own or their families' homes, caring for children at risk through fostering in other people's homes, caring for and resettling ex-offenders within the community – all these have come to be valued in their own right. Those who provide such care often need support. This is where voluntary organizations come in. (Leon Brittan, Speech to the Conference of the NCVO, 5 April 1984)

An important component of the government's attempt to shift the emphasis in service provision away from the statutory sector and on to the community has been the increased role seen for the voluntary sector. Voluntarism accords well with elements of contemporary conservatism: the reduction in state-provided welfare services; the importance of individual initiative; the value of entrepreneurial virtues; the orientation to consumer need, which is assumed when there many providers, and the return to Victorian values – the heyday of the voluntarily organized and provided welfare service. Margaret Thatcher spelt out the links between voluntarism and the wider new-right philosophy in a speech to the Women's Royal Voluntary Service (WRVS), ironically an organization dependent on government funding. She argued that voluntary organizations were of major importance to the maintenance of a free society:

They are not just a way of giving help and caring, vitally important though it is, and the wonderful work which you do; they are an example that we are a free people, and continue to be that and do things our own way. And that when we are free, this is the important thing, we do rise to our responsibilities and carry them out far better than any government. And so I could say that the great volunteer associations are really a vital part of the defence of our freedom of action. There must be a substantial element of private giving if independence of decision is to be maintained. (Thatcher, 1981)

In an apparent rebuttal of the proponents of altruism, the Prime Minister argued: 'Really voluntary work is not fundamentally about generalized good will. It's about individual and continuing effort. It's about doing something one's self' (*ibid.*).

The voluntary sector was important to the government in that it constituted a significant element in the ideological shift of emphasis over welfare provision. Where expectations could be transferred to the voluntary rather than the statutory sector, the nature of entitlement would also undergo a parallel shift. Entitlement from the statutory sector was by right as a citizen; from the voluntary sector it was frequently at the discretion of the giver.

Most of the large voluntary organizations remain in the unelected hands of the great and the good. Politically they have been cautious, notoriously reluctant to engage in aggressive campaigning against the government of the day or to seek, too strongly, to attribute the particular problems experienced by their client groups to any larger social factors. Under the Thatcher government the voluntary sector showed itself willing to collaborate not only in the privatization of parts of the NHS but also in a series of initiatives intended to recruit the unemployed into voluntary activity, with a consequent reduction of pressure on the mainstream social services and a benefit to the unemployment statistics.

The Community Programme and Opportunities for Volunteering inevitably resulted in the increasing involvement of voluntary organizations in the implementation of central government priorities. Unless there should be any misunderstanding of their appropriate role, the Manpower Services Commission enthusiastically policed those organizations in receipt of MSC grants to ensure that they did not engage in any activities which, in the Commission's view, might be deemed political: this might, for example, include activities designed to campaign against high levels of unemployment. A Home Office Minister, Timothy Raison, spelled out the proper role of volunteers when he supported the views of Robert Pinker, in a dissenting note to the Barclay Report on the future of social work, that social workers should stay out of politics:

The argument is that social workers do not serve the interests of their clients by getting drawn into the 'Welfare Rights Industry', community work and community action, including political activities at a local level . . . I think the challenge in these remarks can also apply to the voluntary sector. (quoted in Lawrence, 1983)

In case the 'challenge' was misunderstood, Raison subsequently negotiated with the Home Office-funded Community Projects Foundation to ensure that guidelines were introduced to curb political activity (see *Voluntary Action*, 1983, p. 2).

Not all the supporters of the new right were entirely happy with the growing interrelationship between the state and the voluntary sector. Some saw this as no more than the covert expansion of the welfare state; thus, the Director of the monetarist Social Affairs Unit, Digby Anderson, has argued that there may be a good case for 'stopping the hidden expansion of the welfare state through the *permanent* subsidy of "voluntary" bodies by the central and local state' (Anderson, 1981, p. 19). Sir Alfred Sherman, Deputy Director of the Centre for Policy Studies, a Conservative Think Tank, intervened in the controversy prompted by the decision of Dr Gerard Vaughan, when Minister for Consumer Affairs, to hold an inquiry into the Citizens Advice Bureau before releasing their full government grant. In contrast to those who condemned government intervention, Sir Alfred, speaking to Channel 4 News on 19 April 1983, argued: 'Why inquire only into the Citizens Advice Bureau? Why not the whole new growth industry of so-called voluntary bodies?' (14 April 1983). Sir Alfred argued that the CABs were 'just the tip of an iceberg' of government-funded organizations:

These bodies were voluntary at first. But as years went by, local councils and central government began to make more and more funds available. An open jam pot attracts flies and wasps. These organizations are turning into professional pressure groups demanding more public money for this, that and the other, including themselves and their friends. They are becoming unelected professional politicians. Compassion has become professionalized; indignation provides a livelihood. (*ibid.*)

In practice, the division between the government and its critics may not be as wide as this suggests. In the short term, the funding of the voluntary sector and the accompanying rhetoric provide an important part of attempts to restructure and limit the welfare state. The government has emphasized the importance of the voluntary sector's looking increasingly to the private sector for its support. The then Home Secretary, Leon Brittan, in a speech to the 1984 Conference of the National Council for Voluntary Organizations, argued that the 'success' of the government's economic policy created a particularly favourable climate:

> Company profits have been rising fast. Industrial and commercial companies' profits in 1983 were about 20 per cent higher in real terms than in 1979. The CBI March Survey, just released, is the most optimistic for five years. Companies are under less financial pressure: the time is ripe to approach them with well-thought-out proposals for closer collaboration and greater assistance.

No doubt if this policy could be successfully pursued the return to the virtues of Victorian Britain could be more rapidly achieved. The decisions of corporate directors on the worthy and the undeserving would serve to determine what kinds of welfare programmes the voluntary sector provided. Support for those programmes which sought to reform the character and mores of the deviant poor would be assured. Smaller, genuinely democratic voluntary organizations, which actually represent the clients they serve and which seek to change the social conditions which create the problems encountered by their clients, would receive short shrift. Such organizations, which have received strong support from a number of local authorities, will as a consequence of rate-capping find themselves increasingly marginalized. The voluntary sector will, as government policies are successful, come more and more to represent the government's ideal. It will be a sector firmly in the control of the great and the good, lending its willing support to initiatives further to privatize and dismantle the welfare state and actively collaborating in the larger attempts to 'blame the victim'. Attention will be directed towards the inadequate parenting practices of the poor and not on to the stresses on family life created by poverty and unemployment. Indignation will be mobilized against abusing parents but not against the worshippers of the market and the prophets of inequality.

Privatizing social services

> Twenty-one pensioners are being 'offered for sale' with their old people's home by the London Borough of Wandsworth, which prides itself in extending the frontiers of privatization ... The council is offering a 'dowry' with each resident so the new private owners will receive a guaranteed income from Wandsworth rate payers to look after them until they die. (*Guardian*, 2 May 1984)

The new-right case for reducing state involvement in personal social services and increasing the role of the private sector is similar to the case for dismantling other aspects of state provision. In the particular case of social work it is also linked to attacks on the credibility and worth of social workers and suggestions that their proclaimed professional expertise is largely self-serving and illusory (Brewer and Lait, 1980). Privatization can be achieved in a number of different ways, including the limiting of provision in the public sector to force those wishing to obtain service to turn to the private sector. Services currently provided by the public sector can be contracted out to the private sector and, where there is a viable market, institutions can be sold into the private sector.

Attempts to cut back personal social services encountered strong opposition not only from the government's opponents but also from a number of Conservatives in local government who thought such areas merited special protection. Nonetheless, by ensuring that additional need was increasingly met in the private sector and by increasing the financial pressure on local authorities, the government has secured some shift of resources out of the public sector and into the private sector. This has been particularly notable in the areas of care for the under-fives and for the elderly. Pre-school provision is not a statutory obligation on local authorities and many, including Labour authorities, have sought savings in this area. The consequence has been a growth in private provision of day care, whether in nurseries or through child minders. Government changes in the provision of supplementary benefit to the elderly provided a significant boost to the residential sector, which was already benefitting from the policy adopted by many local authorities of seeking to reduce their capital costs by purchasing places in private establishments. Between 1978 and 1981 the number of over-sixty-fives accommodated in private homes increased by 25 per cent whilst the number accommodated in local authority and voluntary sector homes scarcely changed.

The potential for private sector involvement in day care and care of the elderly is illustrated by the North American experience. Kindercare provides places for 62,000 pre-schoolers in 800 standardized day-care centres in the United States and Canada. Concern has been expressed about the limited and unimaginative quality of the programme offered to the children (Morris, 1984). In commercial terms, however, Kindercare is a major success. Established by a former developer of shopping centres, the company stock on Wall Street rose from $2.25 a share in 1977 to $20 a share by 1984. One of the keys to the company's profitability is its ability to attract staff at exceptionally low rates of pay. Teachers receive on average about $7,000 per year and directors of the centres earn between $10,000-$12,000 per year. The high level of graduate unemployment ensures a continuing supply of staff.

Dependence on low-paid staff also characterizes many of the corporations investing in nursing homes for the elderly. North American profit-maximizing entrepreneurs can seek savings not simply by relying on unemployment to guarantee a supply of low-paid, predominantly female labour, but also on judicious selection and processing of residents. Clearly, elderly residents require different degrees of care depending upon their disability, and it is not uncommon for companies simply to terminate the residential agreement with those who require a level of care which threatens the operator's profitability. Since the nursing homes are seen as a business, like any other, they are bought and sold complete with residents, who may then be required to move to another home owned by the new corporate proprietor. The potential size of this corporate sector is suggested by the 1983 report of the CrownX Corporation, which noted that it 'pursued an aggressive nursing centre acquisition programme' and increased its health-care earnings to 23.4 million, a 66 per cent increase over 1982 (*Toronto Globe and Mail*, 17 May 1984).

Private provision is not confined to the under-fives and the elderly. In the UK there are a number of private residential establishments which cater to the needs of children, often requiring specialist care not available in local authority establishments. Local authorities seeking to reduce their dependence on public sector residential care can employ a dual strategy: increasing the use of fostering whilst placing hard-to-foster children in private sector or voluntary sector homes. There are of course strong arguments against over-dependence on residential care for young people, but the increasing financial constraints experienced by local authorities have led to a policy sometimes described as 'fostering at any cost', but more accurately perhaps as 'fostering at less cost'. The predominance of financial considerations in the move to fostering became transparent with the leaked draft report of a handbook being prepared by the Audit Commission on value for money in the social services. The handbook suggested that authorities fostering fewer than 40 per cent of the children would be challenged on audit grounds and that those fostering between 40 and 60 per cent would be asked to increase their efforts (Laurance, 1984B). The growing emphasis on fostering has increased the role of financial incentives in providing foster parents, and it is reported that some would-be foster parents 'now phone round the London boroughs looking for the best deal', perhaps as much as £150 per week (*ibid.*).

The search for local authority economies has resulted in the abrupt closure of a number of children's homes without any evidence that the local authority has taken seriously its obligation to give full consideration to the welfare of those in its care. Teenage boys in the care of Solihull Council obtained a High Court judgement in their favour when the council sought to close Richmond House. The judge ruled that the council should have considered the welfare of each individual child expected to be in the home by the proposed closing date (*Community Care*, 17 November 1983).

Thatcherite councils also sought opportunities to privatize other aspects of service delivery such as meals on wheels. Experience, as in the NHS, was not always positive. The use of private contractors by Merton Social Service Department to provide meals on wheels and lunches in old people's homes produced a flood of complaints of poor quality. The Secretary of the Social

Care Association described the experience as 'a disaster' (*Community Care*, 2 August 1984). Undeterred, the London Borough of Wandsworth announced that its future plans included a privatization experiment in cleaning and catering services in old people's homes and day centres (*Community Care*, 29 November 1984). Such moves can be justified, as they were by Wandsworth's Director of Social Services, as a necessary means to free revenue for other social service activities. The cost of such changes will be borne not only by those staff whose wages and conditions of work are adversely affected but also by those clients of social services who find that the pursuit of profit has replaced the ethos of public service.

Conclusion

The broader new-right critique of the welfare state predisposed Thatcherite politicians to take a basically sceptical view of both social workers and local authority social service departments. Social workers were often held to be prisoners of those very soft, liberal reform attitudes which were responsible for undermining effort, weakening morality and relaxing those social disciplines required to maintain social cohesion. Local authority social service departments were necessarily suspect in the efficiency of their operations. The government's desire to see the emphasis in care shifted from the statutory sector to the voluntary sector, the community and, in practice, the family, was combined with its continuing attempt to restrict local authority spending to create a bleak future for the personal social services. Social workers might play a useful role in providing scapegoats in child abuse tragedies, in which media attention could be directed not to the cause of child abuse and the dilemmas of local authority social services departments, but to apparent failures in the handling of particular cases.

Social service departments bombarded by clients with increasingly constrained resources were being pushed into a position in which the rhetoric of community care and the shift to 'community social work' disguised an increasing concentration on activities designed to protect the Department's public image. In practice, departments will have little choice but to prioritize resources for high-risk areas, notably child abuse, whilst deflecting the needs of other vulnerable social groups. That in this context social workers should increasingly have been confused over their professional identity and their societal mandate is scarcely remarkable.

Demographic changes and the labour-intensive nature of social services limited the potential economies which the government could achieve within the constraints imposed by local authority control over social service delivery. This lent added urgency to moves to resituate the focus of service delivery into the private sector. There the absence of unionization would serve to curb labour costs whilst standards might be determined by the market with some statutory oversight. The government's announcement, late in 1984, of a forthcoming Green Paper, which would outline plans to contract out to the private sector a range of caring schemes for the elderly, the handicapped and children, gave a stark intimation of the government's future plans.

The ideological argument for a virtually complete state withdrawal from the social services area was continually made clear by the government's supporters. Liverpool University Professor of Economics, Patrick Minford, acknowledged that a problem could arise when families refused to take on the responsibilities of care for their members and felt 'morally justified in abandoning their responsibilities to the state'. Minford recognized that society was unwilling to 'let the victims of this neglect suffer' but suggested that the solution lay in imposing a statutory obligation to provide care rather than in state provision:

> The logical action to take is therefore for such responsibilities to be made legally mandatory, just as child-battering or child-neglect are penalized by the law. Neglect of these family responsibilities would be actionable by the state. (Minford, 1984, XIII)

The imposition of a statutory responsibility to care, together with the growth of a private social-care sector for those affluent enough to afford to use it, would fundamentally reshape British society. Unfortunately for those who share Minford's pre-Cambrian view of society, Thatcherism is unlikely to rule long enough to achieve a full realization of this nightmare.

7. Housing

Housing was a particularly important issue for the new right. The fact that in 1979 some one-third of housing lay in the public sector indicated the scale of the challenge. Housing expenditure had been substantially reduced as a consequence of the Labour government's public sector cutbacks, but in 1978 it still constituted 7 per cent of central government expenditure compared with 12 per cent for education and 12.5 per cent for health and personal social services (Glennerster, 1981, p. 175). Tower blocks provided a convenient, not to say spectacular, example of the apparent inability of the public sector to spend money wisely and to meet people's desires sensibly. The image of public housing became dominated by the tower block and the opposition which was frequently produced by ill-thought-out urban renewal schemes.

Home ownership has a particular salience in British society. The proposal to sell off council housing appealed to free-market purists, to those who already owned their homes and valued this as an important social institution, and to those tenants in the public sector who stood to benefit, particularly those in more desirable terraced and semi-detached council properties with gardens. The sale of council housing would provide a source of increasing government revenue, would extend home ownership, and would tackle the apparently endless maintenance problems in the public sector by making these the responsibility of the new private owners. Pride in ownership, it was hoped, would also contribute to a solution to the social problems which seemed to be concentrated in the public sector.

The 1980 Housing Act offered tenants discounts of between 33 and 50 per cent, depending on their length of tenure, to purchase their own homes. The 1984 Housing and Building Control Act increased the maximum discount to 60 per cent and reduced the initial qualifying period from three to two years, with a 32 per cent discount after only two years. In spite of the pronounced lack of enthusiasm of many Labour local authorities for council house sales, the effect of the legislation was dramatic. By 1984 more than 700,000 public sector homes had been sold, some 11.5 per cent of the total stock (*Guardian*, 12 September 1984). The percentage of owner-occupied homes increased from 54 per cent to 59 per cent during the first Thatcher government, the largest post-war shift recorded (Riddell, 1983, p. 155).

Tenants were encouraged to buy not simply by the discounts offered but also through government policies which shifted subsidies increasingly in favour of mortgage holders. Council house rents more than doubled in the first four years of the Thatcher government. In 1977 subsidies to mortgage holders and council tenants were roughly equal at £141 and £139 respectively (*Guardian*, 4 November 1981). By 1982-83 the subsidy for mortgage holders was around £366 as against subsidies to those in the public sector of around £206 per tenant (Mathews, 1982). The increase in the mortgage on which interest relief could be claimed, from £25,000-£30,000 in that year, further shifted the balance. For tenants, then, it did not simply make good sense to buy a house at a knock-down price, it also became an offer it was expensive to refuse.

The difficulty from the government's point of view was that even with these incentives some tenants could not afford to purchase their own homes, whilst a good deal of public housing stock was almost unsellable. This resulted in very different levels of sales in various parts of the country and for various kinds of property. By March 1982 Bristol had sold over 2,000 dwellings, but whilst flats comprised some one-third of the council stock they comprised only 0.23 per cent of completed sales. West Lancashire had sold 639 of its 4,000 housing stock by the end of 1981; in contrast Tower Hamlets had sold only seven from a total of 18,000 (McDowell, 1983).

For those who couldn't or didn't want to buy their own homes, steep rent increases could have a devastating effect on the family budget. One effect of this was a very rapid increase in rent arrears. The consequence of Energy Secretary Nigel Lawson's imposition of large increases in fuel bills, effectively using energy prices as a means to raise back-door taxation, was that tenants faced a double squeeze. Between 1981 and 1982 rent arrears in Newcastle-upon-Tyne increased by some 50 per cent.

Not surprisingly, given the government's commitment to council house sales, there was a sharp reduction in the amount of new building in the public sector. Housing completions had already fallen from over 160,000 in the mid-1970s to 104,000 by 1979, and by 1982 they had been further reduced to 49,200, the lowest level for more than fifty years (Riddell, 1983, p. 154).

The political benefits to the government of council house sales were clear. Not only did the sales, in common with other sales of public assets, raise revenue and therefore increase the government's freedom to reduce taxes and meet other public expenditure targets, but they also produced an electoral dividend, as Ivor Crewe has shown. Amongst the working class, 57 per cent of council tenants voted Labour in 1983, but amongst working-class home owners the figure fell to 25 per cent. Amongst those who had bought their council houses, 56 per cent voted Conservative and 18 per cent Labour, whilst 59 per cent of those who voted Labour in 1979 and subequently bought their council houses switched to the Conservatives or Alliance (*Guardian*, 13 June 1983).

The advantages of the government's policies were somewhat unequally allocated, for if sales helped the Treasury and the Party's electoral fortunes, as well as benefitting the tenants of better-quality public housing stock, they did little to help those trapped in inner-city high-rises. Indeed, as many commentators pointed out, the inevitable consequence of any policy of council house sales must be to reduce the availability of better-quality housing stock in the public sector. If the sales policy had been part of a comprehensive housing policy which sought to tackle housing shortages, to renovate and replace inadequate housing stock and to bring adequate housing within the reach of all sectors of the population, the results would have been rather different. Revenue from sales could have funded new housing programmes. Indeed, in the context of increasing North Sea Oil revenues, an import boom and high levels of unemployment, there was much to commend a programme which sought to encourage investment in both public and private housing. Such investment would have been labour intensive and its effects predominantly felt in the UK market rather than being dispersed on imports. However, the effect of the recession in the early years of the Thatcher government was to produce a parallel decline in the provision of private sector housing. The new owner-occupiers might largely have joined the comfortable majority but they left behind an increasingly impoverished public sector.

Public housing in Britain, as in the United States, is increasingly becoming housing of last resort. The effect of this change, far from tackling the soical problems experienced in parts of the public sector, will be to produce a further concentration of the deprived and the alienated, locked in public housing ghettoes from which even the possibility of transfer has been ended. One housing expert, looking at the implications of the government's policy, concluded: 'Indeed to reduce public housing to a rump for the socially deprived is the transatlantic recipe for social disaster' (Kilroy, 1982).

It was not simply that council house sales steadily reduced the number of good-quality homes in the public sector but also that local authority cutbacks resulted in escalating problems of repairs and maintenance. By 1985 the Association of Metropolitan Authorities calculated that it would cost £19 billion to repair defects which had been discovered in council houses in England (*Guardian*, 5 March 1985). The government-appointed Audit Commission noted that the backlog of maintenance work on a range of council assets was growing by about £1 billion a year. The Commission noted that renovation would soon become prohibitively expensive (*Guardian*, 15 April 1985).

Many council buildings had been poorly constructed and this, coupled with the neglect of maintenance and repairs, could have fatal consequences. A report in *ROOF* identified a number of fatal accidents consequent upon inadequate construction and poor repairs. The human cost of neglect was illustrated by the case of the three-year-old boy who fell from the sixth floor of a tower block, through a window that had remained unrepaired since being reported as broken three years earlier (*ROOF*, March-April 1984).

In addition to the declining quality of public housing and the reduced choice of tenants as better properties were sold, the impact of government policies was also experienced through a dramatic increase in the number of homeless. The number of households officially recognized as homeless rose by some 50 per cent, from 53,000 in 1978 to 78,000 in 1983 (*Guardian*, 6 November 1984).

The official figures may themselves increasingly under-represent the real number of homeless families. A report in *ROOF* published by Shelter found 'growing evidence' that many families in bed and breakfast accommodation had never been accepted as homeless by the relevant local authority. For example, a survey in Reading of homeless households in which there were children or a first child was expected, living in bed and breakfast hotels, found that 62 per cent had not been accepted by the council as homeless and therefore did not appear in the official statistics (*ROOF*, March-April, 1985).

Again local authorities caught in the vice of central government policies became the focus of hostilities from the government's victims. In the London Borough of Camden, growing pressure on the council's homeless persons section produced first a strike and then an occupation by the homeless families themselves in protest at the appalling conditions in the bed and breakfast accommodation in which, at great expense to the council and enormous profit to the landlord, they had been placed.

Undeterred by these consequences, the government indicated that further cuts would be made both in the funds available for repairs and for new investments. A further fall of 10,000 from the 50,000 homes built in 1983 was anticipated. However, £1.4 million was made available for an advertising campaign advising council and housing association tenants of the increased rights to buy provided in the 1984 Housing and Building Control Act. Such measures could do little to ameliorate the situation of the increasing number of people living in what was described as bed-sitter squalor. This was estimated to encompass some half a million people in 1984. It was estimated that four out of five such properties were substandard and that some 600 people had died in bedsitter fires between 1978 and 1982 (*Guardian*, 24 September 1984).

The government's indifference to the plight of the homeless was given eloquent testimony in its treatment of the single homeless. Far from seeking to make provision for this group, whose number was increasing in size as a direct consequence of the government's economic policies, regulations were introduced which severely limited the entitlement of young people under twenty-six to board and lodging payments. The government also reduced the value of such payments for other claimants. Young people were banned from claiming for more than two weeks in most seaside resorts, four weeks in most towns and cities and eight weeks in London, Manchester and Glasgow (*Guardian*, 10 April 1985). The inevitable consequence of these measures, as Shelter argued, could only be that 'tens of thousands of people would lose their present accommodation' (*Guardian*, 15 April 1985).

The policy of selling council housing, as many Labour politicians recognized, particularly in the aftermath of the 1983 electoral defeat, is unlikely to be reversed. Many of the negative consequences could be avoided by an imaginative programme of new housing construction, not simply in the public sector but through housing associations and co-operatives and other schemes deliberately intended to help the low paid. Indeed, there are good redistributional arguments for supporting housing policies intended to increase the quality of housing owned by low-income groups. Attention should also be given to the situation of those who remain in the private rented sector, which constitutes some 13 per cent of total households. The right to buy, already thoroughly explained and advertised by Conservative politicians, should be extended to private tenants. Legislation could afford some protection to the proverbial widow whilst ensuring that property companies provided the same kind of generous terms to their long-standing tenants as those available in the public sector. If the argument for justifying 60 per cent discounts is that such tenants have already made a substantial investment in their houses, then it is surely equally valid whether the investment was received in the public domain or by private shareholders.

Private affluence from public squalor

The other significant initiative which the Conservative government took in the housing field was to increase the role of the private sector construction industry in the building and maintenance of public housing and other council building work. The 1980 Local Government Planning and Land Act required all house-building contracts above a certain level to be put out to tender. In addition, a proportion of work below that level also had to be placed out to tender and Direct Labour Organizations (DLOs) were required to earn a five per cent return on capital. The act was a boon to the private construction industry which, in response to the depressed conditions in the industry in the 1970s, had launched a major campaign against direct labour. It also reflected the faith of Conservative ideologues in the automatic superiority of the private sector. Thus Councillor Robert Jones was able to assure a seminar organized by the Adam Smith Institute: 'There may be cases of exploitation in the private sector, but every report I read indicates that wages and conditions are better; the people who are joining the new firms are, on the whole, getting more money' (Butler and Perry, 1981, p. 62). In contrast to the alleged profligacy and inefficiency of the DLOs, the private sector, through the operation of market mechanisms, would guarantee a cheaper and better standard of service.

These assertions of faith flew in the face of a great deal of counter-evidence. Most notable was the private sector's record in training, employment conditions, and health and safety. In 1977 local authority DLOs employed 23 per cent of all operatives in the industry but were responsible for training 46 per cent of apprentices and trainees (Secker, 1983, p. 140). The use of 'lump labour' in the private sector was notorious and in general the provision of paid holidays, sick pay and pensions lagged behind the public sector. The number of accidents in the two sectors was also markedly different. In 1980, for example, there were 151 deaths in the construction industry, itself a remarkable figure in contrast with 136 for the whole of the manufacturing industry; only 10 per cent of fatal accidents were in the public sector, in spite of the fact that this accounted for more than 20 per cent of all workers (*ibid.*).

In contrast to the claims made for the superiority of private sector construction lay the fact that a great many of the problems experienced in public sector housing were a consequence of the inadequate workmanship and fraudulent practices which characterized some of the private contractors who built for the public sector. It was frequently difficult for local authorities to get satisfactory compensation from private sector companies for inadequate workmanship and the resultant repairs necessary to bring buildings up to a satisfactory standard, not least because a number of such companies went bankrupt before meeting their obligations.

Problems in construction and repairs, however, were not confined to the private sector. Certainly a number of local authority Direct Labour Organizations were guilty of many of the abuses with which they were charged, including high levels of pilfering, indifferent response to repair demands and an organization of work which seemed primarily designed to accommodate the wishes of those employed. One writer commented on the Walsall DLO:

> Like many DLOs it was rotten from tip to toe. It had incorporated many of the corrupt practices from the private building industry. Like skimping and the manipulation of the bonus system, but they had been exaggerated by complete job security, slack management and the absence of any public service ideology. (Sharron, 1984)

However, as Walsall Council, under Labour leadership, demonstrated, the solution to such problems did not necessarily lie in privatization. Indeed, privatization could well result in such practices continuing, along with the added cost of providing a profit to the company involved and the risk of other corrupt practices designed to increase the size of that profit. Walsall's reorganization and decentralization of its DLO resulted in the first two years in a 120 per cent improvement in productivity, and a very significant improvement in the speed with which repairs were carried out.

The drastic reduction in the amount of housing construction in the public sector, together with the increasing restrictions on DLOs, assured the ascendancy of the private construction industry. The government's ideological conviction in the innate superiority of the private sector guarantees the further erosion of public sector housing and the DLOs. The proclaimed superiority of the market has not, however, prevented the emergence of significant problems in private sector housing, notably the apparent unsaleability of some new housing stock. For those who find that their acquisition of a house has turned into a lifelong millstone, the government has no answer; like the growing number of the homeless and the abandoned residents of inner-city tower blocks, they constitute a stark reminder of the limits of market panaceas.

Education

I am old-fashioned enough to believe that not only is it one's own responsibility rather than that of the state to provide for one's own family, but that, if one is fortunate enough to be able to afford to do so, it is one's right and duty. (Mark Carlisle, Secretary of State for Education, 1979-81)

The new right see education as a major target for policy change, for, like health, it absorbs a significant proportion of the nation's gross domestic product. The dominance of public provision, it is claimed, denies consumer choice (in this case by parents), leads to fewer resources being spent on education than would occur in a free market (Seldon, 1977, p. 77), and results in inefficiency in resource allocation and insufficient attention to the needs of the labour market. As in other public services, 'producer capture' discourages an orientation to meeting consumer need:

Despite the fiction of 'public' ownership, members of the public find that they have virtually no control over state services at all ... An assured income leads to complacency about existing practices and a failure to innovate. Political fears about strikes or unemployment generate lax labour relations and overmanning. Political generosity in wage settlements leads to the (less obvious) trimming of capital replacement. Administrative overheads grow while services often decline. (Adam Smith Institute, 1984, p. 1)

The growth of state education is seen as pre-empting the development of private education which was already well advanced in the nineteenth century:

It seems that even by 1851 two out of three million working class children were receiving some kind of daily instruction. It was, of course, short and inadequate by our present-day standards ... But it was spreading, and by 1870 more children were at school for more years than earlier, and were increasingly leaving later. Moreover, this schooling was entirely voluntary and almost entirely paid for by fees. (Seldon, 1977, p. 63)

This is an important point since it is seen as a refutation of the argument that state intervention was necessary to guarantee the development of education.

There are a number of intrinsic difficulties with these claims. In the UK at least the teaching profession, irrespective of 'producer capture', has been remarkably ineffective in securing high material rewards; indeed, it has experienced the continued erosion of its status. Nonetheless, this argument achieved prominence in 1984 when Sir Keith Joseph, with his almost singular ability to assert ideological fact in the face of empirical reality, blamed teachers' pay claims for the declining state of the educational service, though on teachers calculations their salaries had fallen relative to those of other comparable groups by no less than 32 per cent over the previous ten years.

In fact attempts to control conditions of service and claim areas of professional autonomy are not unique to the public sector; indeed, private sector chartered surveyors provide one example of an occupational group which has been considerably more successful in securing high material rewards, in part on the basis of customary practices and requirements in property transfers, which afford little protection to the purchaser and high rewards to the surveyor. There is no evidence that consumer dissatisfaction has had any effect in restricting this practice. Similarly the claim that, in an exclusively market-run educational system, the teaching profession would both display less concern to pre-empt debate in areas over which it claimed particular professional wisdom and be more willing to engage in genuine partnership with parents, than in the existing publicly provided system, can remain at best in an expression of faith. Existing private sector schools scarcely constitute models of democratic partnership and the consumer remains sovereign only in the sense that where the child meets the entrance requirements and the parents can afford it they may send a child to the school of their choice. If they are subsequently dissatisfied they may move the child. Given the difficulties of doing so, as well as the possible trauma of moving a child from one school to another, some may think this sanction less useful than the ability to write a letter of complaint to a local councillor.

The claim that voluntary fee-paying schools in the nineteenth century provided a satisfactory base for further development ignores the fact that the same service consumers, whose views are held to be so important, voted massively for moves to develop public education. Clearly many in the working and middle classes had a less sanguine view of the future potential of the private education market to meet their needs.

Education vouchers and the education market

The practical problem the new right faced was how to devise policies which would reverse the historical trend to state provision and restore an effective market in education. The vested interests inevitably brought into being by the present system, together with the historically influenced expectations of parents, both militate against the rapid transition to market provision. Any proposed change also needs to take account of the need to minimize the financial cost of moving to a new system, which might be considerable if, for example, the country were suddenly faced with large numbers of redundant public school buildings.

The preferred route of reform has been through the development of an educational voucher. The attractiveness of the voucher proposal is in part its flexibility, in that vouchers could be for full-cost education or could require a parental contribution. Vouchers could be of a determinate value or could be open to parental 'topping up'. Vouchers can also serve as a transitional device in order to pave the way for the acceptability of a full-cost fee-paying system. Thus, as one of the champions of the voucher scheme, Arthur Seldon, proposes:

> The education voucher would be a half-way house to the eventual policy of leaving income with tax payers to use for education. It could gradually be replaced by lower taxes, perhaps over 20 years, as the readiness of parents to buy education was strengthened by increasing knowledge of its benefits (Seldon, 1977, p. 68)

The key attraction of the voucher is that it serves to recreate the market link:

> The voucher would restore the link by giving the parent pur-
> chasing power and thus change him (her) from a recipient of
> 'free' education to a customer who pays for it with money ...
> The whole outlook of the school would thus change. Instead of
> looking to local politicians and officials as a source of its
> money for salaries, books, materials and so on, it would look
> to parents. (*ibid.*, p. 69)

Some even saw the voucher as a mechanism for eroding class differences. Michael McCrum, former head of Eton and Master of Corpus Christi College, Cambridge, neither of them institutions noted for their interest in challenging privilege, argued in favour of the voucher: 'I hope to see our society at peace with itself, not torn apart by class conflict, and the existence of one system of schooling, which would yet allow for real freedom of choice within it, would help to bring about this reconciliation' (McCrum, 1981). In fact, providing those parents who can afford the £5,000-£6,000 needed to send their children to Eton with a £1,000 state subsidy in the form of a voucher might be seen by others as a very good way of exacerbating class conflict.

The idea of vouchers has been largely canvassed as the solution to the perceived problem of state education in primary and secondary schools. For students in further and higher education the introduction of full-cost fees and loans would serve simultaneously to make educational institutions responsive to market pressures, as students became full fee-paying 'customers', whilst providing students with the financial means to do so.

In practice explorations of the voucher system have suggested both financial and political difficulties in implementation, particularly over the short term. The Adam Smith Institute, in a 1984 report, concluded that it seemed unlikely that a voucher scheme would come into effect in the UK.

> The voucher idea involves an immediate, massive, and uncer-
> tain change in school finance. Instead of receiving their funds
> predictably from governmental bodies as at present, all schools
> would have to become competitive over night ... While this
> may bring the undoubted benefit of choice to parents, and

would make education at an independent school an option available even to the poorest, it unifies the educational establishment against it ... The crucial problem with the idea is that it cannot be subject to experimentation in any effective way: acceptance must be all or nothing. It is therefore unlikely to happen. (Adam Smith Institute, 1984B, p. 16)

The Institute therefore turned its attention to alternative measures which might aid the transition towards a more market-oriented educational system.

The Institute suggested that tax rebates, of say £500, offered one way forward so that parents educating their child at an independent school would be entitled to a rebate of some proportion of the cost that would otherwise have been incurred in educating the child in a state school. Obviously one immediate implication of the scheme would be an immediate transfer of funds into the hands of those whose children are already in the private sector. Apparently, however, this is not the case:

> Despite the enigmatic *prima facie* appearance that the rebate is simply a subsidy to the better off, in fact it is just the reverse. If a better-off family sends its children to a state school, it costs the tax payer about £1,500 per year per child. But if that family instead chooses to go independent and take the rebate, the net cost to the tax payer is only £500 or so per child per year. If it is assumed that the principal uptake of the scheme will be better-off families, then it actually represents, in sum, a shift of resources away from the better-off. (*ibid.*, p. 18)

This tunnel-vision reasoning ignores the fact that many of the beneficiaries will not previously have been receiving any rebate, with the exception, of course, of the various tax shelters, charitable perks and rate relief advantages which the private schools and their patrons have enjoyed under successive governments. The proposal does, however, like the Assisted Places Scheme, have the advantage of providing a more gradualist approach to change.

The introduction of increasing cash incentives, however provided, would serve to reduce the cost of private education to parents and must extend the size of the market and hence increase the acceptability of private education and the pressure for further change. The major drawback to the scheme, from the point of view of a government concerned with containing public spending, is that in the short term its introduction will be disproportionately expensive in terms of the numbers affected since, as has been suggested, the major immediate beneficiaries will be those parents whose children are already at independent schools. The providing of financial support to these particular parents will not of course reduce the pressures on the state system and will therefore create no compensatory saving.

One other proposal from the Adam Smith Institute deserving mention is the suggestion that an amount of money might be set aside from the educational budget and given to local businessmen to allocate between schools:

> Thus, local businessmen would use the sum to support schools they believed were producing good students. This could be achieved by giving the main local businesses a certificate they could award the schools individually, and which was encashable by the school against government funds; or simply to organize a poll of local businessmen and distribute a number of awards centrally on the basis of returns. (*ibid.*, p. 21)

The Institute argues that such a programme would tackle the problem that 'employers have no say in education decisions'.

This 'finding' would come as something of a surprise for the large number of employers sitting on local education authorities (LEAs) across the country, not to mention the failure to acknowledge the efforts of such well-known educators as James Callaghan and Lord David Young to ensure that employers' views are more than fully represented.

Another influential monetarist, Patrick Minford, in a blueprint for cutting back public expenditure, has simply suggested selling off the schools: 'The schools system could be sold to private firms in diverse "lots", and not necessarily all at once, but rather spread out over the transition. Or even longer (Minford, 1984, p. xii). The solution to the political difficulties would be found in gradualism:

> The problem of transition is therefore one of ensuring political acceptability by changing gradually . . . The fiscal effects of these plans are obvious enough. State expenditure on

education is assumed to be phased out over the five-year transitional period, saving £3.5 billion in 1985-86 and the full £16 billion from 1990 onwards. (*ibid*.)

Whether the inhabitants of Merseyside, who surround the ivory tower from which Minford delivers his manifestos, would see this five-year period as being sufficiently gradual, must be a question of individual judgement.

Choice, selectivity and comprehensives

The new-right approach to education was based, in part, on a strong attack on the way in which the public education system in Britain had developed. Comprehensives were seen as having eroded standards, encouraged the growth of large schools which boosted career prospects for staff without any equivalent educational advantages, and, in the name of social justice, stunted the development of more gifted children. The rapid growth of post-secondary education was thought to have resulted in a frontal assault on standards. These views were well expressed in Sir Keith Joseph's major speech in Birmingham in 1974 in which he argued for the importance of choice in education and pointed to the decline in educational standards:

> When we oppose the imposition of a uniform state monopoly over education, it is not for the sake of privilege but, on the contrary, in order that the area of choice can be widened and made available to more citizens, that the talented children of the poor may have the best education in the environment best suited to them. We are opposed to using children as guinea pigs or spare parts for social engineers to experiment with. We are opposed to any policy that denies to parents the right to spend their own money on their children's education if they so choose. (*The Times*, 21 October 1974)

Sir Keith believed that parents should be free to choose 'in spending their money on better education and health for their children instead of on a new car, leisure, pleasure . . . ' (*ibid*.). Sir Keith did not specify what kinds of automobiles or pleasure he had in mind but given the cost of private education the first would have had to have been luxurious, to say the least, and the second exotic. In 1981, for example, a boarding place in the average public school cost about £4,000 and, as the *Daily Telegraph* noted, 'that is just for basics' (*Daily Telegraph*, 8 March 1982). Since more than half the population would have been required to spend some 50 per cent of the family income in order to avail themselves of this choice for even one of their children, for most people the choice must have been constrained, to put it mildly.

For those who 'choose' to educate their children in the state system, Sir Keith's description of that system must have caused some concern. Sir Keith argued that the removal of responsibility from parents to the state, and the growth of public spending, had exacerbated social problems, a situation for which the education system clearly must accept part of the blame:

> We were taught that crime, violence, wife-beating, child-beating were the result of poverty; abolish poverty, and they would disappear . . . By now, we are in a position to test all these fine theories in the light of experience . . . Real incomes per head have risen beyond what anyone dreamed of a generation back; so have education budgets and welfare budgets; so also have delinquency, truancy, vandalism, hooliganism, illiteracy, decline in educational standards. Some secondary schools in our cities are dominated by gangs operating extortion rackets against small children. Teenage pregnancies are rising; so are drunkenness, sexual offences and crimes of sadism . . the decline is spreading. We know that some universities have been constrained to lower their standards for entrants from comprehensives, discriminating against the more talented because they come from grammar or independent schools . . . If equality in education is sought at the expense of quality, how can the poisons created help but filter down? When young people are taken away from their home milieu, in late adolescence, crowded together in age groups, with diminished parental and indeed, adult influence, and without social disciplines which the need to earn a living impose, is it surprising that their late adolescent rebelliousness should feed on itself and seek ideological rationalisations? Left-wing ideology is so convenient for this purpose, it requires little knowledge and less analytical thought, it is the compendium of all-purpose phraseology

... Some will carry on and extend their adolescence as teachers in schools and polytechnics and in universities helped by the like-minded, where they will cooperate with the left-wing gangs. But worse still is the effect of these winds of change in the schools, particularly in poorer districts among less gifted children, and in social work. (*The Times*, 21 October 1974)

This denigration of state education and its alleged contribution to the general decline in moral and cultural standards in society remained a prominent new-right theme, reinforced by contributors to the Black Papers on education, and by the indefatigable efforts of writers like Carolyn Cox (elevated to the peerage by Margaret Thatcher) and John Marks, to challenge the academic quality of the comprehensives as measured by examination performance. It was also a prominent theme for the newly formed Social Affairs Unit at the Institute of Economic Affairs.

The Unit's second publication, *Educated for Employment?*, aptly illustrates the relationship between such publications and the mobilization of political opinion on education. An article by Walton in the *Times Higher Education Supplement* summed up the intellectual calibre of the contributions:

Unmonitored standards, self-interest, waste, drunkenness, violence? Members of the Social Affairs Unit begin after a while to sound like beleaguered Conservatives armed with ideological riot guns. Their scatter shot criticism does only indiscriminate damage and singularly fails, so far, to bring down any real targets. (Walton, 1982)

This conclusion is amply justified by any analysis of the contents of the publication (Loney, 1983). Nonetheless, for the editorialists on the *Daily Telegraph*, the publication serves to substantiate the new-right critique by providing insider confirmation. An anecdotal account of further education provides damning evidence:

The picture is of a field where competence is neither common, nor rewarded. Pay and promotion are little associated with merit, demotion and sackings are almost unheard of. Classes are stated in statistics to be very large, so that cuts may be avoided, but in practice those attending them are a far smaller number ... Defects in Further Education are partly attributable

to the mediocre ethos of much vocational teaching, encouraged by the semi-Marxist orthodoxies which regard work in
industry or business as a subject for medical treatment, rather
than a worthwhile way of earning a living . . . The consequences for the economic success of the nation . . . are very bad.
(Editorial, 26 May 1982)

The *Daily Telegraph* thus uses this insubstantial pamphlet as a
jumping-off point for proclaiming the empirical truth of the
argument of 'producer capture' and proceeding to suggest that
this is directly related to Britain's economic decline. This in turn
confirms the view that youth unemployment may be largely attributable to the negative attitudes, inadequate education and inap-
propriate skills of young people.

Claims about the low standards achieved by comprehensive
schools and the general denigration of public sector education
were accompanied by the growing assertion that educational
resources were largely irrelevant to educational outcomes. Students of social mobility had long since drawn attention to the
close links between social class and educational achievement. Sir
Keith Joseph's skill lay in turning this argument into a justification for declining educational expenditure. Under his direction,
the DES produced figures to demonstrate that different levels of
exam success by pupils in different local education authorities
could be largely explained by the difference in home backgrounds, and not by the difference in local authority per capita
expenditure. Hence, although Buckingham spent only a little
over two-thirds of the resources per pupil of the Inner London
Education Authority, its A-level attainments were twice as good
(*Times Educational Supplement*, 14 December 1984). The data on
the link between social class and educational mobility had largely
been used to argue the need for more broadly egalitarian social
policies. In the hands of the Thatcher government, such data now
provided support for cutbacks in educational expenditure.

Similar arguments have been current in the American right for
some time. In a 1971 article, leading neo-conservative, Irving
Kristol, argued:

There is practically no correlation between the physical plant
of our schools and the academic achievement of our students.
Middle-class parents who think they are improving their

children's academic potential by sending them to a brand-new school with a fine library, sumptuous gymnasium, a lovely lunch room are kidding themselves. So are slum parents who think that their children's academic potential is weakened by old buildings ... What determines a child's academic achievement is his genetic endowment plus the values and motivation he acquires at home. Even class size turns out to have nothing to do with academic achievement. (Kristol, 1973, p. 145)

In many ways the indictment of the left and the right is similar; however, the conclusions drawn are different. Left-wing critics have been far more willing to spend additional sums on education in the hope of achieving some minor amelioration of the situation. In addition, they have sought to develop programmes which might overcome the negative impact of home background whether by increasing expenditure on pre-school education or by seeking to improve home and school links. Essentially for the right, the indictment is not of a class society but of those amongst the poor who have failed sufficiently to motivate their children to succeed. Kristol has argued, 'As such poor families move up the economic and social ladder, as their home life becomes more stable and the family concern for education becomes more emphatic, the student's academic performance improves' (*ibid.*, p. 147).

The government's record

Government policy unfolded against a background of declining enrolment in schools, which enabled the government to cut educational spending whilst claiming to be responsible for a marginally improved pupil-teacher ratio. In fact the cuts in the educational budget and the difficulty LEAs experienced in making rapid adjustments to declining school roles resulted in significant cutbacks in provision. In 1975 spending on education had accounted for 6.25 per cent of GNP; by 1982 it had fallen to 5.25 per cent, and the government envisaged a further decline to 4.50 per cent of GNP by 1986-87 (Hughes, 1984, pp. 21-2). Whilst the government sought to exercise control over the level of spending on education, much of the dissatisfaction with the effects of local cuts could be directed against local education authorities. Here, as in the Health Service, government sought to suggest that problems were caused not by central government policies but by local extravagance, inefficiency and unproductive bureaucracy.

The government used a variety of approaches to cutting spending on education, including limiting access (notably to universities), putting pressure on local authorities to cease spending on items which were not seen as educational (such as school meals), and encouraging schools to raise funds directly from parents. In some areas charges were increasingly used to finance 'non-essential' parts of the curriculum, notably sports and music. A number of education authorities introduced charges, but a High Court judgment against Hereford and Worcester, over the charging of fees for music tuition provided within school hours, provided a setback. Section 61 of the 1944 Education Act requires that 'no fees shall be charged in respect of ... the education provided in any (maintained) school' (Redhead and Doyle, 1984, p. 28). Nonetheless, the judgment failed to settle the matter since it left it open to education authorities to eliminate particular provisions altogether, to charge for lessons outside school hours or to find other forms of deterrent. In Hereford and Worcester it was reported that about 5,500 children were learning a musical instrument before the ruling, 800 under individual tuition. By 1983 the number had halved, with very few taking individual lessons (*Times Educational Supplement*, 4 February 1983). Hereford and Worcester reportedly provide free swimming lessons but they are available only to those children whose parents pay the coach fares to the baths; all the children are obliged to travel on the coach, but those who don't pay the fare sit out the swimming session (Bull, 1983, p. 56). The effects of such practices on those for whom choice is not a question of replacing the Range Rover or having Priscilla educated privately, but rather of putting food on the table or sending money to school, hardly needs spelling out.

The government's enthusiasm for parental contributions was expressed fairly quickly. In 1980 Mark Carlisle, Secretary of State for Education, told the National Association of Head Teachers that there was no reason why parents shouldn't be allowed to pay for essential books. No doubt inspired by this patriotic sentiment, teachers in a Solihuss comprehensive sought to levy £3 per head per term on parents to purchase books (*ibid.*, p. 54). Parental contributions became commonplace and by 1984 it was estimated that some 15 per cent of books in state schools were being bought by parents (*Guardian*, 23 April 1984).

Parents were not only called upon to purchase books but, increasingly, local education authorities looked to parent-teacher associations to organize fund-raising for other forms of provision, including libraries, the costs of running computers and equipment needed for school courses. Financial contributions from the LEA could be conditional upon contributions from parents (Pring, March 1983). The situation in Wales was summarized by Mr Lyn Clement, Chairman of the Welsh Secondary Heads Association, who described the position in the biggest authority, Dyfed:

> In this country there are school departments which are only being kept going by what parents give, particularly materials to craft and woodwork departments. In trying to meet the changes in A level syllabus introduced by the Welsh Joint Education Committee young pupils are suffering. They are doing without text books or sharing them, three to a copy. I would call that critical. (*Times Educational Supplement*, 13 December 1984)

The 1984 school inspectors' annual report noted that across the country three out of four schools described parental contributions as 'modest' or 'substantial'.

The government also sought to introduce a means-tested charge for school transport in the 1980 Education Act, but this measure was defeated in the House of Lords. It is nonetheless open to LEAs to make charges to those pupils using school transport who live within the defined 'walking distance'.

The school meals service had already been undermined by cuts introduced by the previous Labour government and by the initiative of local Conservative-controlled education authorities. In 1976 the Labour Chancellor indicated that he intended to halve the 62 per cent school meals subsidy by 1980, and in 1977 the price of a school meal was raised from 15p to 25p. LEAs were encouraged to find ways of cutting costs, such as introducing convenience foods and reducing staffing levels (Glendenning and Dixon, 1983).

The 1980 Education Act abolished the statutory obligation on local authorities to provide school meals to all children. The legislation permitted local authorities to provide school meals, but it obliged them only to provide meals for children whose parents were in receipt of supplementary benefit or family income supplement. In addition, facilities had to be provided for children bringing their own food. Prices and nutritional standards for meals were no longer determined nationally. The consequences of government policies and the new legislation were quickly apparent. The quality of meals provided declined. Prices of meals increased and the number of children taking school meals declined dramatically. Many school meals employees lost their jobs or faced cuts in wages and conditions of service.

Privatization was also experimented with by a number of Conservative local authorities but in general private contractors were unable to match the in-house cost of providing meals. The appointment of an outside contractor at Clacton County High School in Essex, for example, cost the council £2,000 more than the estimate of the in-house service. In a nearby primary school attempts to privatize had to be abandoned when private tenders were five times higher than the county's calculation (*Times Educational Supplement*, 20 August 1982).

The victims of government policy were not only those children who were faced with meals of declining nutritional standard or who could no longer afford school meals, but also the low-paid employees of Conservative county councils. A number of these, led by Devon, Somerset and Kent, broke the national agreement covering pay, holiday retainer fees and meals, effectively sacking staff who would not accept reduced pay and conditions (Bickerstaffe, 1984).

Some local education authorities simply closed down parts of the service. Dorset, Lincolnshire and Hereford and Worcester abandoned the service in the primary schools. Children eligible for a free meal received a centrally packed cold lunch (Glendenning and Dixon, 1983).

The government's parsimony towards the state system was in marked contrast with its generosity to the independent system, which benefitted from the introduction of the assisted-places scheme. Inflation in school fees and the impact of the recession on parents had left a number of independent schools in a parlous financial situation, with inadequate demand for the available places. The assisted-places scheme provided a major boost. It is estimated that in 1988 at least 142 schools will have more than one in five of their students financed under the scheme (*Guardian*, 10 February 1984). By 1984 the scheme was already costing £22.5 million per year, with a projected continuing increase in government expenditure. The programme no doubt assisted the slow growth in the proportion of students in the independent sector, which rose from 5.6 per cent in 1978 to 6.2 per cent in 1983 (*New Society*, 10 May 1984).

The pressure to introduce a scheme of educational vouchers continued throughout the period of the first Thatcher government. Voucher schemes were considered by civil servants in the Department of Education and Science and were actively promoted both by Sir Keith Joseph and by Dr Rhodes Boyson. However, in spite of various press reports which suggested that voucher proposals were about to be presented, none publicly surfaced. Political, financial and administrative difficulties left various schemes stillborn.

The Central Policy Review Staff paper on public spending, which caused considerable controversy when it was leaked in September 1982, rejected the idea of vouchers. The paper suggested that these could actually increase public spending as a consequence of offering vouchers to those parents whose children were being educated privately. One option which the paper suggested instead was the introduction of charging for all schooling (*Education*, 24 September 1982).

The government's failure to privatize the primary and secondary education system led, as in the Health Service, to a search for areas which might at least be contracted out. Although there was little success in contracting out the provision of school meals more was achieved in the contracting out of school caretaking and school cleaning. Here, in common with the experience in the NHS, privatization frequently ignored the less quantifiable aspects of the job. The thought that cleaners and caretakers, who saw themselves as part of the educational service, might have a different attitude towards their work than those who worked for private sector contractors had clearly not occurred to business-oriented local councillors. Victims of their own rhetoric about the sloth and indifference of public sector workers, they found the instrumental attitude of private sector contractors could create serious difficulties. Merton Borough Council had to terminate its contract after only a few months. The council acknowledge that many classrooms were 'not fit to teach in' and that 'a storm of complaints had been received' (TUC, 1984, p. 20). A report for Dudley Council admitted that under private contracting 'the general standard is still far lower than the service previously provided by direct labour cleaners' (*ibid.*, p. 12).

Contracting out was part of a broader attempt to achieve economies and reflected a general decline in standards of maintenance. In Birmingham, for example, the number of hours per week allocated to cleaning 50 large secondary schools was 21,543 in 1975 and 12,662 in 1983. In that year, an unsuccessful bid by the Council's Direct Labour Organization to secure the new contract further reduced the figure to 7,685 (*ibid.*, p. 4).

The fall in standards was not the only negative consequence of privatization; here, as in the Health Service, wages and conditions were quickly eroded.

Further and higher education

The new-right objective was to transform the further and higher education sector into one financed by full fee-paying students, supported by loans. The reality was of a declining resource base for the universities, a gradual erosion of the level of student grants and an increase in parental contributions. The introduction of a student loan scheme remains as one possibility, albeit as a backup to reduced student grants.

The Central Policy Review Staff (CPRS) paper on public spending envisaged an end to state funding of higher education; the charging of all students full-cost fees, estimated at £4,000 for an average three-year course; the provision of means-tested state scholarships to 300,000 students, and the provision of loans to another 200,000 students (*Education*, 24 September 1982). These proposals were rejected, and Sir Keith Joseph's subsequent attempt in 1984 to introduce tuition fees of up to £520, payable by students who were ineligible by virtue of the means test to receive any state grant, ran into overwhelming opposition from backbench Conservative MPs. The government's supporters had been prepared to accept increases in council house rents, reductions in the real level of benefits, declining access to health services and reduced income for the low paid as a necessary price for economic recovery. A suggestion that parents with residual incomes in excess of £19,000 per year might make a contribution to the tuition fees of their children produced uproar. Keith Hampson, Conservative MP for Leeds North West, drew attention to the plight of the 'upwardly thrusting lower middle classes' whom Mr Hampson believed were those with a joint income of £20,000 (*Guardian*, 7 December 1984). Hermione Parker, a leading critic of the supposed work disincentive effect of high benefit levels, offered an agonized description of the new 'poverty trap' into which the £17,000 per year family was to be placed as a consequence of the increased parental contribution (Parker, H., 1984).

Nonetheless Sir Keith's success in slowly eroding the value of the student grant and increasing the parental contribution will increase the acceptability of loans. The government has secured the *de facto* acceptance of a lower state involvement in financing higher education. The introduction of top-up loans would simultaneously reduce pressure on parents and ease the problem of students facing inadequate grants, and might therefore meet the test of political acceptability. Once loans are introduced, the way would be open to increase their importance in financing post-secondary education.

Nonetheless, the significance of the U-turn over student tuition fees should not be underestimated. From a monetarist perspective the arguments for transforming higher education into an independent, privately financed system are impeccable. Such a change, it is claimed, would transform students into consumers who are conscious not simply of the quality of their education but also of its relevance to the labour market. Full-cost fees would force universities to act in a business-like fashion and calculate the real costs of their different degree programmes. The Adam Smith Institute even raised the question of the equity of the existing system, arguing 'it is unclear why young building workers should pay higher taxes so their contemporaries can spend three or four years, with free subsistence, at a university that probably has vast land holdings, and qualify for a better-paid job in the process' (Adam Smith Institute, 1984B, p. 29). Indeed, access to universities is profoundly unequal. In 1982 the 62 per cent of the eighteen-year-old population at the lower end of the Registrar General's social class scale – skilled occupations, manual, partly skilled occupations and unskilled occupations – provided only 18 per cent of successful university entrance candidates (Association of University Teachers (AUT), 1983, p. 18).

In retrospect it may be that it was precisely the disproportionate advantage that higher-income groups gained from state expenditure on higher education which ensured such a vehement opposition to proposals to reduce state financing in this area. Market forces and the minimal state may be all right for hospital cleaners, but not for well-heeled Conservatives and their supporters. Here, as in the Health Service, the government's rhetoric was not matched by any even-handed application of free-market principles.

The overall effect of government cutbacks to the universities was that by 1984 some 20,000 fewer places were available. The cost of compensating redundant staff amounted to some £66 million (*Guardian*, 16 May 1984). In 1979, 53.9 per cent of qualified home applicants were accepted; by 1982 the figure had fallen to 46.4 per cent (AUT, 1983, p. 20). These cuts took place in spite of the fact that the UK retained a lower proportion of its students in higher education than most other western industrial countries.

Many disappointed university students went into the polytechnic sector, but the combined effect of increased pressure on the polytechnics, in the context of restricted resources, and severe cutbacks in the university sector could only be to diminish the quality of education. In pursuit of supposed greater efficiency, a large number of university academics were offered attractive redundancy packages which frequently ensured that those with marketable skills in business, accountancy, law or geology received large financial inducements to leave the public sector and accept the more attractive salaries already on offer in the private sector. A further consequence of these financial restrictions was an increasing difficulty in recruiting new staff in key areas, notably in the field of computing and information technology. The announcement in 1984 of plans to construct a new privately run institution, linked to Cranfield Institute of Technology, to train experts in these fields, may foreshadow broader changes in training in such areas.

The development of business-backed and business-controlled educational institutions would constitute a marked shift in the control of further and higher education curricula in the UK. It would, however, parallel developments which have been taking place in the educational field in the United States and provide an alternative route through which government involvement in higher education could be reduced and through which key areas could be protected from the consequence of government cutbacks. The way would then be open both for teaching staff to be paid on different scales depending upon whether they were in the public or private sector, and for low-resource art, social science and general science courses to predominate in the public sector.

The government gave a boost to the private sector of higher education by granting a Royal Charter to University College at Buckingham. The university was founded with the clear ideological commitment to operate outside the state system. The granting of the Royal Charter caused some controversy. An editorial in the *Times Higher Education Supplement* noted that with 470 students, more than half of them from overseas, teaching in a limited number of subjects and little institutional research, the university was scarcely comparable to existing universities. Noting the contradiction between Buckingham University's desire for independence and its eager pursuit of a Royal Charter the editorial concluded: 'The simple truth is that Buckingham should never have been granted a Royal Charter and, more important perhaps, it should never have asked for one' (25 February 1983).

Government ministers encouraged state universities to seek private sector financial support, a move which was in any case necessitated by the declining availability of government funds. Universities also responded to the marked increase in foreign student fees by actively seeking to recruit an increasing number of such profitable customers.

Some concern was expressed about the implications for academic freedom of increasing dependence upon business funding and funding from other non-UK government sources. The development of Arab studies at Exeter University, for example, was largely dependent upon Arab funding. Elsewhere other universities sought and obtained generous foreign financing for departments devoted to study of the country in question. The questions which such foreign sponsorship raise are also posed when the study of accountancy, industrial relations or management is increasingly financed from corporate resources.

In pursuit of foreign students, London's City University reportedly decided to admit overseas students with just two 'C' grades for the study of business computing systems, whereas home students required at least two 'B' grades and one 'C' grade at A-level. The London School of Economics, eager to adapt to market forces, dealt with the difficulty that some of the increasing number of foreign students had in obtaining post-graduate qualifications by introducing new qualifications. As one commentator noted, '...the LSE has established special less academically demanding lower-level diploma courses for them. Thus the School avoids embarrassment both to itself and to the students who, having paid substantial fees, have failed their courses' (Bradley, 1983, p. 7).

There is still of course some way to go before British universities adopt the practice of some American universities and simply sell degrees by mail. Nonetheless, there was some concern at the apparent resurfacing of nineteenth-century values in Oxford when it was discovered that Wadham College had accepted £500,000 from a Hong Kong businessman who had been offered places for two of his children. The *Guardian* noted that Parliament had banned the buying of Oxbridge places more than a hundred years ago and argued, '...it is an interesting reflection of current government education policy that what would have looked like a corrupt threat to university standards in 1870 can be presented as a good business deal ... more than a century later' (11 March 1982).

Academic freedom, local democracy and central control

Sir Keith Joseph's strong views on education were backed by an increased level of government intervention in the content of education.

Sir Keith had always had a particular suspicion of the social sciences. As Secretary of State at the DHSS in the Heath government, he had jointly commissioned, with the Social Science Research Council, research into transmitted deprivation. Sir Keith was a strong believer in the idea that poverty and the deviant behaviour of the poor were transmitted by family patterns. As Sir Keith told the Pre-School Play Groups Association in 1972:

> It seems perhaps that much deprivation and maladjustment persists from generation to generation through what I have called a 'cycle of deprivation'. People who are themselves deprived in one or more ways in childhood become in turn the parents of another generation of deprived children. (Rutter and Madge, 1976, p. 5)

The failure of subsequent research to confirm Sir Keith's view did not produce any public reversal of his position. It may well, however, have contributed to his growing distaste for social science research, particularly as many of the researchers in the joint programme suggested that what was needed was broader political and economic change:

> Much of the research concerned with very broad definitions of deprivation has inevitably concluded that disadvantage is deeply rooted in the structure of our society. Explanations not only of poverty but even of poor health or child abuse are concerned to emphasize the importance of the uneven distribution of income and wealth in our society, of the unequal structure of employment opportunities, of the class-related pattern of life chances in terms of morbidity, educational achievement and even personal happiness. (Brown and Madge, 1982, p. 6)

One of Sir Keith's first acts as Secretary of State for Education was to appoint Lord Rothschild to lead an inquiry into the work of the Social Science Research Council. Sir Keith was particularly animated by the use of the word 'science' in the council's title, preferring himself the phrase 'social studies'. It was believed that the inquiry was intended to pave the way for the council's abolition (*Times Higher Education Supplement* editorial, 28 May 1982). In fact, the subsequent report was generally sympathetic to research in the social sciences and recommended that there be no reduction in the SSRC's budget in real terms. Nonetheless, Sir Keith imposed a £6 million cut on the council. In response to government pressure, the SSRC was subsequently retitled the Economic and Social Research Council. The subsequent appointment to head of the council of Sir Douglas Hague, for many years a supporter and confidante of the Prime Minister, completed Sir Keith's reforms.

This was not, however, the end of Sir Keith's forays against the social sciences. He next sought to give ministerial backing to allegations of bias against the Open University's introductory social sciences course. Sir Keith's interest in the university's social science programme occurred in a situation of the university's experiencing growing financial pressure through government cutbacks. A report commissioned by Sir Keith Joseph from a group of professional economists sought to substantiate the allegations of bias, though since the economists appeared unable to distinguish between Marxists and Keynesians too much weight should not be placed on their findings (Loney, 1984). The Open University, whilst rejecting the claims, announced a number of changes to the course and significantly increased outside vetting to ensure 'balance'. More importantly Sir Keith had signalled to other academics that he thought the detailed content of higher education a matter for ministerial intervention.

The government's attempt to exercise increasing influence over the curriculum is not confined to higher education. The abolition of the Schools Council removed one source of progressive and hence undesirable influence over the educational agenda. The creation of a new DES-appointed curriculum council will vastly increase central control over the content of education.

Sir Keith, in conjunction with Lord Hugh Thomas, prior to Thatcher a mere Professor of History, has advocated the creation of a common history curriculum. Sir Keith has argued: '... one of the aims of studying history is to understand the development of the shared values which are a distinctive feature of British society and culture and which continue to shape private attitudes and public policy' (Purdue, 1984, p. 49). This contentious proposition overlooks considerable evidence which suggests a diversity of values and attitudes, and a degree of conflict; indeed, what is at stake is no more than an attempt to assert that certain prized Conservative values are the national values. Hugh Thomas has argued that post-war collectivism failed because 'it ran against our national traditions of self-reliance and independence' (Thomas, 1983).

There are very considerable dangers in the moves to articulate a centralized history curriculum. What this may mean in the

British context is that the impact of radical historians such as Christopher Hill, A.J.P. Taylor and E.P. Thompson will be cast to one side while the new curriculum will provide a more sanitized view of British history, in keeping with the notion that that history is not about conflicts of class, race and gender but 'the development of shared values'. In contrast with the attempts to fit the teaching of history into the context of a multi-cultural society, Lord Thomas has suggested: 'There are a lot of immigrants here, and they need to get a sense of the country they live in' (Walker, 1983).

The government's main instrument in seeking greater control of the educational curricula in secondary and further education was the Manpower Services Commission. The appointment of Sir David, soon to be Lord, Young to head the Commission continued the pattern of politicizing key appointments. Young, whose brother was appointed to chair the Board of Governors of the BBC, was a friend of the Prime Minister from her Finchley constituency, and in 1984 was promoted to the Cabinet.

As the government cut back resources for internationally respected university degrees, the Manpower Services Commission stepped up funding of courses in further education. David Young made his own philosophy abundantly clear: 'Training should not be confused with education. Training is about work-related skills and is intimately concerned with employment. It is for this reason that training in this country must be employer dominated and ultimately employer led' (*The Director*, October 1982). Although the MSC has produced no evidence to suggest that it has had any effect on increasing the amount of work available to young people, in spite of the expenditure of many millions of pounds, the government proposed further extensions of the Commission's role in a 1983 White Paper, 'Training for Jobs'. This continued the vocational thrust which appears to attribute youth unemployment, in some measure, to an absence of relevant training: 'The public sector needs a greater incentive to relate the courses it provides more closely to the needs of the customer in the most cost effective way'. The customer is clearly private sector industry, and the White Paper turned its back on any notion of meeting the social educational needs of the young unemployed.

The MSC's obsessional concern to exclude any whiff of politics from the courses which it finances severely restricts their content and provides one clue to the kind of educational changes under way. In view of the fact that many young people are destined to remain unemployed, there is a strong argument not only for providing an adequate social education for young people on MSC courses but also for ensuring that the causes and consequences of unemployment are discussed. In the absence of such discussions, effectively precluded by the MSC, young people may well, in line with the prevailing government views, blame themselves: for having no skills or the wrong skills, for lacking motivation, for interviewing poorly, for living in the wrong region, or for not taking up cycling more energetically.

The growing role of the MSC was of course exercised at the expense of democratically elected locally accountable councillors. Increasingly, MSC finance provided the carrot which pulled the educational system in the direction in which the government wished it to move.

The future pattern of centralization will depend in part on the political complexion of local authorities. Where local authorities are unsympathetic to the government's broader policies, their freedom of action will be increasingly confined by rate-capping. Ironically, the crisis in educational financing, the decline in standards, and the cutbacks and industrial disputes which this could produce, may lead to popular hostility being misdirected to those local authorities caught in the central government's vice.

The MSC, having established its credentials through a series of highly cost-effective schemes whose unifying theme is their ability to remove the unemployed for some period of time from the official statistics, seems assured of further support. It provides central government with an opportunity simultaneously to outflank local authorities and to ensure that increasing areas of the educational curriculum are suitably sanitized.

Conclusion

The educational legacy of the Thatcher government will be found in a school system which, in the face of growing unemployment, was directed to expend its efforts on an ever-narrower vocational curriculum: a curriculum based not only on the philistine proposition that all activity must ultimately be subservient to the pursuit of Mammon, but also on an approach to the philosophy of education which certainly predated Plato. And a curriculum which failed to confront the social needs of those destined for the dole.

Cutbacks at all levels of education left a growing backlog of maintenance work, poorly resourced classrooms and demoralized teaching staff. The government had failed to introduce the radical innovations which its ideologues had hoped for. Private education had made only limited gains, whilst voucher schemes no longer seemed credible. At post-secondary level the government had failed to introduce any real market mechanisms; rather, the pursuit of austerity minimized innovation and eroded educational quality. Increasingly it seemed that the only consistent thread in the government's educational policy was that expenditure should be reduced.

9. Wasted Years

What an achievement is hers! She has persuaded the nation that everything that goes wrong, from unemployment to the crime rate, is an Act of God or someone else's fault; that the forces of organised labour are actually the enemies of organised labour; that we can only defend ourselves by giving the United States the power of life and death over us; that to be an 'activist' is somehow far worse than being an inactivist, and that the left must once more be thought of in Latin, as sinister. She propounds what is in fact an ideology of impotence masquerading as resolution, a con-trick, and it looks as though it's going to work: Maggie's sting. (Rushdie, 1983)

In the first half of 1984 investment by manufacturing industry was still 25 per cent below what it had been in 1979. North Sea oil has been used to finance not our convalescence but our euthanasia. (Gilmour, 1984)

The supporters of monetarism had claimed that harsh measures were necessary in order to restore the profitability and productivity of the British economy. Welfare had to be cut in order that the private sector economy could flourish. Inequality was a necessary price which must be paid to unleash enterprise. Monetarists might therefore reasonably dismiss the indictment of the government's social policies on the grounds that these had created the preconditions for economic regeneration; indeed, if the Chancellor, Nigel Lawson, and his supporters were to be believed, government economic policy had done no less. In fact, a more measured reading of the first five years of the Thatcher government would indicate not an economic recovery but an unprecedented waste of economic resources. As North Sea oil production hit its peak, the government succeeded not in using the opportunity to revitalize Britain's admittedly undercapitalized manufacturing sector, but in presiding over a situation where Britain, in 1983, became for the first time in 200 years a net importer of manufactured goods.

The importance of North Sea oil to Britain's economy is indicated by the fact that by 1984 the North Sea oil industry accounted for somewhere between a quarter and a third of the country's business profits (HMSO, Regional Trends, 1984).

The government, in addition to its failure to utilize North Sea oil revenue to restructure the British economy, also engaged in the large-scale sale of public sector assets. Like North Sea oil revenue, the income from such sales was simply spent in financing tax cuts and reducing the public sector borrowing requirement. A household analogy, of the kind popular with the Prime Minister and her supporters, might compare this to the sale of furniture in order to pay this week's rent. In fact the situation was somewhat worse than this, since the average householder, compelled to sell furniture, could be expected to look for the best price. In selling public assets the government systematically under-priced those assets sold into the private sector. More than £1.5 billion was lost on British Telecom alone, whilst overall the privatization programme constituted a massive resource transfer from the state to the affluent.

It is perhaps a fitting tribute to the Thatcherite grasp of economics that at a time when Britain was desperate for new investment in manufacturing, large amounts of available cash should have been soaked up by the privatization of public assets. Future generations will have cause to ask quite how a government was able to use finite national energy resources and sell off public sector assets without leaving any legacy other than spiralling unemployment and a growing crisis in Britain's manufacturing industry. The loss of profitable public sector assets means that future governments will be denied this income whilst any renationalization will constitute a major public sector expenditure burden.

Not surprisingly, monetarists, who in common with other true believers have shown scant interest in evidence which cast doubt on their faith, suggested that what was needed to extricate Britain from its deepening economic crisis was a more rigorous application of the same. Given the infallibility of monetarist theory it was necessary to produce some other scapegoat to account for Britain's economic decline. This was quickly located in the figure of the overpaid British worker who, monetarists argued with increasing insistence, was simply pricing himself or herself out of work. The Chancellor, Nigel Lawson, referred enthusiastically to the decline in real earnings in the United States and argued that this was a key factor in the US economic recovery and in particular in its employment record. This, he argued, 'has been almost entirely due to the more efficient, competitive, innovative and adaptive labour and goods markets in the United States . . . Relatively free markets, the spirit of enterprise, and workers who prefer to price themselves into jobs rather than out of them, are a powerful engine of employment' (Lawson, 1984).

In America, unions cover only 18 per cent of the workforce, and an already patchy benefit structure has been further eroded by the Reagan administration. Whether similar wage reductions can be imposed on the highly unionized British workforce in the context of a developed and, more importantly, popularly supported welfare state, remains to be seen. Even if such policies were successful the consequences are by no means clear. The reduction in wage levels and welfare spending in America went hand in hand with a spiraling federal deficit which fuelled economic demand. In the UK such reductions in benefits and wage levels could well reduce aggregate demand and further contribute to Britain's economic decline. In any case the social price which would be paid for a continuing growth in inequality needs to be offset against any claimed economic advantages. In the United States the enterprise economy has gone hand in hand with inner-city dereliction on a scale unparalleled even in the worst areas of Liverpool and Glasgow, and with a national homicide rate eight times that of the UK.

Monetarism has not only failed to live up to its promises on the economic front but it has also failed to achieve the remoralization of British society. The doom-laden speeches of Sir Keith Joseph in 1974, which bemoaned the declining standards in society, and the Conservative Party's strong emphasis on law and order in the 1979 election, appeared to offer the prospect, under Conservative leadership, of a declining crime rate and increased adherence to traditional values. In fact in the first three years of the Thatcher government, serious crime increased by 30 per cent whilst, although there was a 9,000 growth in the number of police officers, the detection rate fell from 42 per cent in 1978 to 37 per cent in 1982. The dramatic growth in heroin abuse, which reached epidemic proportions in some inner-city areas, constituted a very visible testament to the government's failure to provide the stability and social cohesion which the new right had promised. Indeed the individualistic ethos of contemporary conservatism, coupled with dramatic increases in unemployment, undermined the sense of social solidarity which had provided some protection to deprived working-class communities.

The police, increasingly aware of their inability to control the rise in crime or to improve their detection rate, placed renewed emphasis on their public order role. Sir Kenneth Newman, Chief Commissioner of the Metropolitan Police Force, a force with the worst detection rate in the country, gave some indication of this thinking in a 1983 lecture, in which he indicated the areas which gave greatest concern:

> Throughout London there are locations where unemployed youth – often black youths – congregate; where the sale and purchase of drugs, the exchange of stolen property and illegal drinking and gaming is not uncommon. The youths regard these locations as their territory. Police are viewed as intruders, the symbol of authority – largely white authority – in a society that is responsible for all their grievances about unemployment, prejudice and discrimination. They equate closely with criminal 'rookeries' of Dickensian London ... If allowed to continue locations with these characteristics assume symbolic importance and negative symbolism of the inability of the police to maintain order. Their existence encourages law breaking elsewhere, affects public perceptions of police effectiveness, heightens fear of crime and reinforces a phenomenon of urban decay. (Gilroy and Sim, 1985).

The policing of the miners' strike reflected the growing politicization and centralization of police control. The social conflicts generated by Thatcherism became the primary target of police activity. Indifferent for years to the racial harassment and intimidation of Asians in their own homes in the East End of London, the Metropolitan Police Force was nonetheless able to deploy thousands of officers to defend the right of a handful of miners, in distant countries, to cross picket lines. Police forces unable to make any impact on heroin epidemics on their own doorstep sent thousands of officers into South Yorkshire where they were used, amongst other things, to storm the pit village of Armthorpe. The brutality and illegality of much of the police behaviour in the coalfields attracted widespread comment, though not from the government. One freelance photographer, working for the Italian press, commented on the events that he witnessed at Armthorpe: 'Units of six police cornering innocent passers-by; people mistaken for pickets, being severely beaten; police blatantly entering houses without any reasonable suspicion; housewives and children on a nearby council estate being inexcusably abused. The list, I can assure you, is endless' (Rodrigues, 1984).

The shift from a welfare society to a law and order society can be graphically illustrated. In 1979, the Health and Social Services budget was parallel to that of defence. In 1985, £1.5 billion more was spent on defence. In 1979, £600 million more was spent on defence than on education. By 1988, government figures indicate that £5.2 billion more will be spent on defence. In 1979, the housing budget was nearly twice the size of the law and order budget. The situation, by 1985, had been reversed (HM Treasury, 1985).

The new right had offered a different and decisive alternative to the pragmatic 'muddling-through' tradition of British politics. In fact the consequence of the pursuit of specifically ideological solutions to Britain's postwar decline was to accelerate that decline. At a time when North Sea oil had given Britain a relative international advantage, the policies of the Thatcher government ensured that Britain suffered greater recessionary pressures than other western countries. By 1984 the government had more than doubled the number of those receiving supplementary benefit. OECD calculations of standardized unemployment rates for the developed world showed Britain to have a significantly higher level of unemployment than most of its competitors. Figures for 1984 showed Britain's rate at 13.4 per cent as compared with 8.6 per cent in Germany, 9.1 per cent in France and 7.3 per cent in the United States. The average for the developed world was 8.2 per cent (*Guardian*, 30 November 1984).

The government's commitment to monetarist dogma was well illustrated in its attitude towards the value of sterling, which it allowed to rise by more than 40 per cent from 1979 to 1981, with disastrous consequences for the competitive position of British industry. The rise was due to a combination of Britain's North

Sea oil and the market's infatuation with Thatcherism. The government, believing that the market must be pre-eminent, did nothing to prevent the damage that this inevitably caused to Britain's manufacturing industry. Those who survived being carried under by the cheap imports and expensive exports consequent upon sterling's strength were, by 1985, threatened by sterling's weakness as the government, again in response to market forces, raised interest rates in an attempt to prevent the continuing fall in sterling's value. With confidence in Britain's economy declining, and oil a less certain source of support, government policies seemed destined to buy temporary support for sterling at the price of continuing industrial decline.

10. The future of welfare

The government's antipathy to the welfare state remained unabated. Its major problem, politically, was that its policies remained constrained by the public support for most welfare measures, particularly spending on health, education and pensions. In the context of the government's declining electoral popularity, the desire of leading Thatcherites to inflict a fundamental reversal on the welfare state during their second term seemed unlikely to be realized. The social security reviews, the continued attacks on housing benefit, the additional pressure placed on the education service by the government's refusal to meet teachers' pay demands, the further staffing cuts in the Health Service ordered by the new 'managing director' Victor Paige, and the cuts in lodging allowance and entitlement to benefit for those under twenty-six indicated that the government was nonetheless prepared to proceed against the welfare state by attrition.

The ideological attack against the welfare state remained strong, yet it became more difficult for the advocates of market panaceas to maintain the offensive in the face of mounting evidence of the government's failure to tackle Britain's economic and social problems. Indeed it is arguable that it was precisely the government's failure to tackle the massive increases in unemployment or even to suggest that it had any viable long-term strategy to deal with unemployment that constituted the achilles heel of the government's social programme. It would have been far easier for government supporters to sustain the charge that the unemployed had had their incentive to work stifled by overly generous welfare benefits if their status were not so clearly a consequence of the government's economic policies.

The fact that in cutting back the welfare state the government was frequently inflicting further punishment upon those who were already the victims of its economic policies became increasingly transparent. The argument that such cutbacks would put Britain back to work could scarcely be expected to continue to convince. Nonetheless, the government's traditional supporters did what they could. As the government prepared to launch the findings of the social security reviews, the popular press turned its attention again to the supposed benevolence of the British welfare state. Under the banner headline 'Better Off on the Dole', the *Daily Express* advised its readers that 'a family man on average earnings might just as well be on the dole' (24 April 1985). The *Express* claimed that official figures showed that a man with two children earning £150 per week has 'virtually the same spending power in work or out' (*ibid.*). This gallant attempt to raise the threshold for the impact of the so-called 'poverty trap' was based on the simple expedient of juggling with a series of figures to reach the required conclusion – irrespective of their validity. Thus, for example, it was assumed (although the *Express*'s readers were not informed of this) that in the case of the unemployed, both the husband and wife were benefitting from the £4 per week disregarded income, thereby raising the family spending power by £8. In fact DHSS statistics show that only 1.3 per cent of men and 12 per cent of women have part-time earnings.

If monetarism had provided an effective model for the rejuvenation of Britain's economy its social philosophy would have gained immeasurably in credibility. In contrast, it was the very failure of monetarist economics which stimulated increased demand for welfare services and provoked a greater sympathy for the increasing number of people who were cast in the role of claimant.

The publication of the Green Paper on the reform of social security and housing benefit confirmed the government's continuing commitment to eroding welfare entitlements whilst avoiding the political costs of a full-scale assault on the welfare state. The social security reviews heralded the gradual phasing-out of the state earnings-related pension scheme (SERPS) and significant but unspecified further reductions in housing benefit. The phased abolition of SERPS simultaneously offered a boost to the private insurance industry. Employees would in future have to pay a minimum of four per cent of income into a private pension scheme.

The proposed introduction of a new family credit scheme, based on an assessment of net rather than gross income, was intended to ensure that the reduction of benefit in response to rising income would not exceed the actual rise in earnings. This step, which was intended to ameliorate the impact of the poverty and unemployment traps, and ensure that those in work would never be worse off than those out of work, appealed to a central aspect of Tory mythology. However, the Green Paper failed to make clear what the real rate of marginal tax would be on recipients of the new family credit. Such calculations would have required some assessment of the cost of the proposals and the probable benefit levels. This would have necessarily indicated the magnitude of the overall anticipated losses to welfare recipients. In turn, this would have increased the government's vulnerability to further attacks for seeking to increase the hardship of the poor. Nonetheless, early indications were that the government envisaged significant savings, including £500 million in housing benefit alone, much of which would be borne by the poorest claimants (*Guardian*, 5 June 1985).

The government's problem was that having come to power without any mandate for the radical reform and curtailment of the welfare state, it had, by its own policies, increased the need for welfare measures. The pursuit of monetarist economics and the deification of market remedies had meant growing social inequality, massive unemployment and a deliberate encouragement of the low-wage sector of the economy. To proclaim the importance of fostering a greater spirit of self-dependence and a return to 'doing for one's self' at precisely that moment when increasing numbers of people were being rendered dependent scarcely constituted a recipe for political success.

Arguments about the virtues of private health insurance or the value of private education would have been given greater force if the economic climate had actually facilitated continuing expansion in these areas. Instead, the government presided over a deteriorating NHS and a visibly rebellious public educational system. The private sector remained marginal to national need and a victim of the low growth rate and high unemployment which denied it any significant increase in clients. The rich under the Thatcher government may have got richer, but they failed to increase in numbers at anything like the requisite level. The financial squeeze experienced by other sectors of the population denied them the opportunity to join in the expansion of private welfare, even had they shared the desire to do so.

In its broader desire to restrict the role of government in society, the Thatcher administration was equally constrained by the consequences of its own socially divisive policies and the growing levels of disorder in deprived areas in Britain. In response to soccer hooliganism, the government insisted that this was a matter for the football clubs to deal with. The police force, which demonstrated a singular ability to stop the movement of miners around the country during the coal strike, was apparently unable to stem the exodus of armed thugs to continental football matches. Only the tragedies at Bradford and Brussels forced the government to retreat from its properly monetarist, ostrich-like posture and acknowledge, with continuing expressions of reluctance, that it would have some role to play. The fact that the violence had moved from a localized expression in sports grounds and communities where it predominantly affected the working class to the international stage undoubtedly played some role. As the British elite jetted around the world, at least some of the ramifications of Britain's continuing decline could scarcely be ignored.

Soccer hooliganism may have represented the most visible and ghoulish expression of Britain's social tensions but it was by no means the only one. The police having discovered during the miners' strike that the use of violence and illegality in pursuit of government objectives produced commendation rather than censure applied themselves to public order with renewed zeal. In February 1985 a large and initially peaceful demonstration in Central London in support of the miners resulted in 121 arrests and a number of vicious police assaults. The GLC publication *Policing London* reported: 'One man was dragged along the ground, and his leg trapped underneath a parked car. The police yanked him free so violently that his leg was twisted 180 degrees and broken in two places' (April-May 1985).

Hippies, intending to celebrate the summer solstice at Stonehenge in defiance of a court order, were subject to massive police retaliation when they attempted to break through a police barrier on the public highway. Vehicles seized by the police were reportedly wrecked *after* being impounded. One of the travellers who protested at this deliberate destruction of the impounded vehicles was reportedly given a 'kicking' and required hospital treatment (*Guardian*, 10 June 1985). Amidst the predictably sensationalist coverage, it was left to the travellers' spokesman, Sid Rawles, to draw out the connection between rising unemployment and the search for an alternative lifestyle dependent neither on work or the consumer society (World This Weekend, Radio 4, 11 June 1985.

The steady attrition of welfare provision, the virulent attacks on the victims of the government's policies and the growth of an increasingly brutal authoritarianism were marks of Thatcherism's continuing impact. Nonetheless, a strategic victory continued to elude the government. At the end of the government's second term the welfare state may be weaker, its resources more thinly stretched, its beneficiaries less generously treated, its undeserving groups more punitively appraised, but it will nonetheless continue to constitute a considerable feature on the British landscape. This is a measure of the government's failure but, in concluding, we should return to the government's legacy:

Epitaph

During its first six years the Thatcher government achieved the increasing polarization of British society, the impoverishment of large numbers of the population, a catastrophic decline in Britain's manufacturing industry, the alienation of hundreds of thousands of young people with no prospect of work, and the continuing attrition of the nation's health, education and welfare services. Simultaneously the government proclaimed that the new national philosophy should be based not on altruism but the eager and unfettered pursuit of self-interest: the politics of greed.

Bibliography

Abel-Smith, B., 'The Cost of Health Services', *New Society*, 12 July 1979.

Abel-Smith, B., *Cost Containment in Health Care*, London: Bedford Square Press 1984.

Adam Smith Institute, *Social Security Policy*, 1984A.

Adam Smith Institute, *Omega Report, Education Policy*, 1984B.

Anderson, D., *Breaking the Spell of the Welfare State*, London: Social Affairs Unit 1981.

Arnold, B., *Margaret Thatcher, A Study in Power*, London: Hamish Hamilton 1984.

Ashton, P., *New Society* Letters, 5 April 1984.

Association of University Teachers (AUT), *The Real Demand for Student Places*, 1983.

Avery, L., 'The Super-Snoopers' Claims to Savings that Don't Add Up', *Guardian*, 6 September 1982.

Beckerman, W., *Pricing for Pollution*, Hobart Paper 66, Institute of Economic Affairs, 1975.

Behrens, R., 'The Conservative Party From Heath to Thatcher', in *Policies and Politics, 1974-79*, Hampshire: Saxon House 1980.

Berry, D., 'Licence to Drug Addicts', *Guardian*, 22 February 1984.

Bickerstaffe, R., 'School Meals: A Service Eaten Away', *Poverty*, August 1984.

Board of Inland Revenue, *International Comparisons of Direct Tax on Employment Income*, 1984.

Bosanquet, N., 'The Americanization of the Labour Market', *Poverty*, December 1983.

Bosanquet, N., 'Social Policy and the Welfare State' in Jowell, R. and Airey, C. (eds), *British Social Attitudes, The 1984 Report*, Hampshire: Gower 1984.

Boyson, R. (ed), *Down With the Poor*, London: Churchill Press 1971.

Boyson, R., *Parental Choice*, London: Conservative Political Centre 1975.

Bowling, A., 'Caring for the Elderly Widowed – the burden on their supporters', *British Journal of Social Work*, Vol. 14, 1984.

Bradley, P., *Undue Influence, Pressures on the Universities*, Occasional Paper No. 2, London: Centre for Contemporary Studies 1983.

Brewer, C. and Lait, J., *Can Social Work Survive?*, London: Temple Smith 1980.

British Dental Association, *NHS Dental Treatment, What it Costs and How the Cost has Risen*, 1983.

Brittan, S., 'The Economic Tensions of British Democracy', in Tyrrell, Emmett Jr. (ed), *op. cit.*

Brown, M. and Madge, N., *Despite the Welfare State*, London: Heinemann 1982.

Bull, D., '"Free" Education: Shirking and Shifting Responsibilities', in Bull, D. and Wilding, P. (eds), *op. cit.*

Bull, D., and Wilding, P. (eds), *Thatcherism and the Poor*, London: CPAG 1983.

Butler, E. and Perry, M., *Economy and Local Government*, Adam Smith Institute, 1981.

Coetzee, S., *Flat Broke: How the Welfare State Collapsed in Birmingham*, Birmingham: Birmingham Welfare Rights Group 1983.

Cohen, P. and Anderson, G., 'Mopping Up the Unions', *New Statesman*, 18 May 1984.

Collier, J., *Lancet* Letters, 1 December 1984.

Community Care, 22-29 December 1984.

Comptroller and Auditor General, *Housing Benefit Scheme*, London: Her Majesty's Stationery Office 1984.

Conservative Central Office, *The Conservative Manifesto*, 1979.

Corrigan, P., 'Popular Consciousness and Social Democracy', Marxism Today, December 1979.

Cosgrave, P., 'The Failure of the Conservative Party, 1945-75', in Tyrrell, Emmet Jr (ed), *op. cit.*

Coulter, P., 'Why the Sting Hit the Wrong Target, Background', *Community Care*, 23 September 1982.

Cowling, M. (ed) *Conservative Essays* London: Cassell 1978.

Crawford, A., *Thunder on the Right: The New Right and the Politics of Resentment*, New York: Pantheon 1980.

Deacon, A. and Bradshaw, J., 'Reserved for the Poor: the means test', in *British Social Policy*, Oxford: Basil Blackwell and Martin Robertson 1983.

DHSS, *Child Abuse: A Study of Enquiry Reports, 1973-81*, 1982.

Donnison, D., 'Social Policy: An egalitarian view', *Community Care*, 11 October 1984.

Driver, C., 'How the Poor Eat', *New Society*, 22 November 1984.

Duke of Edinburgh, 'Intellectual Dissent and the Reversal of Trends', in Seldon, A. (ed), *The Coming Confrontation*, London: Institute of Economic Affairs 1978.

Egginton, J., 'Who Loves New York?' *Observer*, 24 May 1981.

Fimister, G., 'Insurance Benefits: From Neglect to Assault', in Bull, D. and Wilding, P. (eds), *op. cit.*

Finch, J. and Groves, D., 'Community Care and the Family: A Case for Equal Opportunities', *Journal of Social Policy*, Vol. 9, Part 4, October 1980.

Fitzgerald, T., 'The New Right and the Family' in Loney, M. *et al (eds), op. cit.*

Flew, A., *Education, Race and Revolution*, London: Centre for Policy Studies 1984.

Forsyth, M., *Re-Servicing Britain*, London: Adam Smith Institute 1981.

Forsyth, M., *Re-Servicing Health*, Adam Smith Institute 1982.

Franey, R., *Poor Law, The Mass Arrest of Homeless Claimants in Oxford*, London: CHAR, CPAG *et al.* 1983

Friedman, M., *Capitalism and Freedom*, Chicago: University of Chicago Press 1962.

Fusco, L., Letters, *Health and Social Services Journal*, March 1982.

Galbraith, J.K., 'Our Debt to Ronald', *New Statesman*, 25 November 1983.

Gamble, A., *Britain in Decline*, London: Macmillan 1981.

Gilder, G.F. *Sexual Suicide*, London: Millington 1973.

Gilder, G.F., *Visible Man: A True Story of Post-Racist America*, New York: Basic Books 1978.

Gilder, G.F., *Wealth and Poverty*, London: Buchan & Enright 1982.

Gilmour, Sir Ian, 'Why Market Forces are Not Enough', *Guardian*, 26 September 1984

Gilroy, P. and Sim, J., 'Law, Order and the State of the Left', *Capital and Class*, February 1985.

Glendenning, C. and Dixon, P., 'School Meals: Privatization, Stigma and Local Authority', in Bull, D. and Wilding, P. (eds), *op. cit.*

Glennerster, H., 'Social Service Spending in a Hostile Environment', in Hood, C. and Wright, M., *Big Government in Hard Times*, Oxford: Martin Robertson 1981.

Golding, P. and Middleton, S., *Images of Welfare*, Oxford: Blackwell, 1982.

Griffith, B., 'How to Ensure Against Good Health', *New Socialist*, July/August 1984.

Gummer J.S., *The Permissive Society*, London: Cassell 1971.

Harrington, M., *The Other America: Poverty in the United States*, London: Penguin, 1963.

Harrington, M., 'The New Gradgrinds', *Dissent*, Spring 1984.

Harris, R., 'The Complaisant Economy', in the Institute of Economic Affairs, *Crisis '75 . . . ?*, London 1975.

Harris, R., *The End of Government . . . ?*, London: Institute of Economic Affairs Occasional Paper 58, 1980.

Harris, R. and Seldon, A., *Over-ruled on Welfare*, London: Institute of Economic Affairs 1979.

Hart, D., 'Time to Sell Off the NHS', *The Times*, 5 December 1983.

Hayek, F.A., *Law Legislation and Liberty: Vol. 1 – Rules and Order*, London: Routledge & Kegan Paul 1973.

Hayek, F.A., *Law Legislation and Liberty: Vol. 2 – The Mirage of Social Justice*, London: Routledge & Kegan Paul 1976.

Hayek, F.A., 'Beware the Weasel Word', *The Times*, 11 December 1983.

Hencke, D., 'Pulse of a Service', *Guardian*, 23 April 1983.

Henkel, H.A. and Pavelka, F., 'Abuse and Social Welfare Policy: A Critique of Strategies for Limiting Welfare State Benefits', *Euro-Social Newsletter*, No. 25, Vienna: European Centre for Social Welfare 1982.

Howe, Sir Geoffrey, 'Agenda for Liberal Conservatism', *Economic Affairs*, January 1983.

Howell, R., *The National Health Service, Facts and Solutions*, London: Aims of Industry 1983.

Hughes, J., 'The Inequality of Impoverished Education', *Poverty*, August 1984.

Huhne, C., 'Why Milton's Monetarism is Bunk', *Guardian*, 15 December 1983.

Huhne, C., 'Thatcherism May Work in the House, But Not in Britain', *Guardian*, 14 February 1985.

Jay, P., 'Englanditis', in Tyrrell, Emmet Jr (ed), *The Future that Doesn't Work*, London: Doubleday 1977; *Guardian*, 14 February 1977.

Jensen, A.R., 'How Much Can We Boost IQ and Scholastic Achievement?', *Harvard Educational Review*, 39, Winter 1969.

Johnson, P., *The Recovery of Freedom*, Oxford: Basil Blackwell 1980.

Johnson, P., 'The Real Crisis Facing the Tories', *Daily Mail*, 10 October 1983.

Johnson, R.W., 'Russia After Andropov', *New Society*, 16 February 1984.

Jones, I., 'Medicine is Infected by Egalitarian Politics', in Seldon, A. (ed), *The Litmuss Papers – A National Health Disservice*', London Centre for Policy Studies 1980.

Jones, P., 'Pay Bed Veto', *Guardian* Letters, 30 May 1984.

Judge, K., Smith, J. and Taylor-Gooby, P., *New Directions in Social Policy? Public Opinion and the Privatization of Welfare*, Discussion Paper 268, Personal Social Services Research Unit, University of Kent, 1983.

Kaldor, Lord, 'Wasted...On an Overseas Posting', *Guardian*, 2 May 1984.

Keegan, W., *Mrs Thatcher's Economic Experiment*, London: Allen Lane 1984.

Kellner, P., 'Labour's Wilderness Years', *New Statesman*, 30 October 1981.

Kemp, J., *An American Renaissance: A Strategy for the 1980s*, New York: Harper & Row 1980.

Kilroy, B., *The Times* Letters, 29 May 1982.

Kristol, I., *On the Democratic Idea in America*, New York: Harper & Row 1973.

Kristol, I., *Two Cheers for Capitalism*, New York: New American Library 1978.

Labour Research Department, *Privatization, Who Profits?*, 1983.

Lait, J., 'Elusive Goal of Total Health', *Daily Telegraph*, 22 December 1983.

Lansley, S. and Weir, S., 'Towards a Popular View of Poverty', *New Society*, 25 August 1983.

Laurance, J., 'Are We Getting Value for Money from the Health Service?', *New Society*, 26 August 1982A.

Laurance, J., 'Private Advantage', *New Society*, 27 May 1982B.

Laurance, J., 'The Collapse of the BUPA Boom', *New Society*, 24 February 1983.

Laurance, J., 'The Eyes Have It', *New Society*, 16 February 1984A.

Laurance, J., 'Taking Care', *New Society*, 3 May 1984B.

Lawrence, R., 'Voluntary Action: A Stalking Horse for the Right?', *Critical Social Policy*, Vol. 2, No. 3, Spring 1983.

Lawson, N., 'The British Experiment', The Fifth Mais Lecture, London: Treasury Press Office 1984.

Layton-Henry, Z., 'The Tories: In Two Minds Over Race', *New Society*, 24 August 1978.

Lekachman, R., *Greed is Not Enough, Reaganomics*, New York: Pantheon 1982.

Leigh, D., 'Immigration Takes on a Marginal Influence', *Guardian*, 4 March 1978.

Leonard, P., 'Restructuring the Welfare State', *Marxism Today*, December 1979.

Levi, M., 'The Powers of Revenue Agencies: An Overview', *British Tax*

Review, No. 1, 1982.

Lewis, P., 'The Evil Of Poverty Among Wealth', *Community Care*, 21 June 1984.

Lipset, S.M. and Raab, E., 'The Election and the Evangelicals', *Commentary*, March 1981.

Lister, R., 'The 1983 Budget', in Bull, D. and Wilding, P. (eds), *op. cit.*

Loney, M., Review in *Youth and Policy*, Vol. 2, No. 2, 1983.

Loney, M., 'A Sinister Farce', *Times Educational Supplement*, 27 July 1984.

Loney, M., Boswell, D. and Clarke, J. (eds), *Social Policy and Social Welfare*, Milton Keynes: Open University Press 1983.

Low Pay Unit, *Unequal Fringe Benefits*, 1984.

Lynes, T., 'Family Roulette', *New Society*, 11 October 1984.

Macmillan, H., 'The Middle Way', 20th Anniversary Speech to the Conservative Political Centre, 1966.

McCrum, M., 'The Voucher: A Pep-pill for Schools and a Cure for Society', *Education*, December 1981.

McDowell, L., 'The Sale of Council Houses, A Case Study of Policy Change' (Course D355), Social Policy and Social Welfare, Open University, 1983.

McLachlan, G., Introduction in McLachlan, G. and Maynard, A. (eds), *The Public/Private Mix for Health*, Nuffield: The Nuffield Provincial Hospitals Trust 1982.

Marsland, D., 'Wage Councils Destroy Jobs', *Economic Affairs*, January 1984.

Mathews, R., 'Rent Asunder', *New Society*, 18 November 1982.

Meacher, M., 'Britain's Failing Health Policies', *Guardian*, 20 July 1984.

Minford, P., 'State Expenditure: A study in waste', *Economic Affairs*, April-June 1984.

Moore, C., 'Mr Fowler's Blackboard', *Spectator*, 11 June 1983.

Morris, B., 'The Ready-wrapped Child Minder', *The Times*, 21 March 1984.

Mueller, C., 'In Search of a Constituency for the "New Religious Right"', *Public Opinion Quarterly*, Vol. 47, 1983.

NALGO, *Profit Out of Health*, Birmingham and Solihull Health Branch of NALGO, 1983.

New Society, 'Social Trends, How Britain's Wealth is Shared', 17 September 1981.

New Society, 'Reagan's Joy and Misery Index', 3 May 1984.

Nissel, M. and Bonnerjea, L., *Family Care of the Handicapped Elderly: Who Pays?*, London: Policy Studies Institute 1982.

Novak, T., *Poverty and Social Security*, London: Pluto Press 1984.

Office of Health Economics, *IHE Compendium of Health Statistics* (5th edn), 1984.

O'Higgins, M., 'Privatization and Social Security', *Political Quarterly*, May/June 1984.

Oldfield, C., 'The NHS' in Hastings, S. and Levie, H., *Privatization?*, Nottingham: Spokesman 1983.

Open University, 'Joan Robinson on Monetarism', Teaching cassette for Social Sciences: a foundation course, 1982.

Owen, D., *Face the Future*, London: Jonathan Cape 1981.

Parker, H., 'Sir Keith's New Poverty Trap', *New Society*, 6 December 1984.

Parker, P., 'Health Care Reaganomics', *Marxism Today*, November 1984.

Paul, J., 'Contracting Out in the NHS', *Critical Social Policy*, Summer 1984.

Penn, H. and Simpson, R., 'State of Seige', *New Society*, 12 April 1984.

Pollitt, C., 'Inequalities in Health Care' (Course D355), Social Policy and Social Welfare, Open University, 1983.

Pond, C., 'Politics of Envy', *New Society*, 9 September 1982.

Pond, C., 'Britain Out of Step', *New Society*, 22 November 1984.

Policy Studies Institute, *Supplementary Benefit, New Evidence*, 1984.

Poverty, *Poverty Diary*, Winter 1984.

Pring, R., 'Privatization', *Where*, No. 186, March 1983.

Purdue, A., Re-writing History', *Salisbury Review*, October 1984.

Quine, L., 'Alone in the Community', *New Society*, 11 June 1981.

Readhead, G. and Doyle, N., 'Protecting the Free Curriculum', *Poverty*, August 1984.

Riddell, P., *The Thatcher Government*, Oxford: Martin Robertson, 1983.

Rodrigues, P., *Guardian* Letters, 10 December 1984.

Roll, J., 'Facts and Figures' *Poverty*, August 1984.

Royal Commission on the Distribution of Income and Wealth, *An A-Z of Income and Wealth*, London: Her Majesty's Stationery Office 1980.

Rushdie, S., 'She Has Persuaded the Nation that Everything Which Goes Wrong is an Act of God', *Guardian*, 23 May 1983.

Rutter, M. and Madge, N., *Cycles of Disadvantage*, London: Heinemann Educational 1976.

Scruton, R., *The Meaning of Conservatism*, Harmondsworth: Penguin 1980.

Scruton, R., 'Left, Right: Putting Things Straight', *The Times*, 6 December 1983.

Scull, A., *Decarceration, Community Treatment and the Deviant: A Radical View*, New Jersey: Prentice-Hall 1977.

Secker, J., 'The Construction Industry', in Hastings, S. and Levie, H., *op. cit.*

Seldon, A., *Charge*, London: Temple Smith 1977.

Seldon, A., *Whither the Welfare State*, Institute of Economic Affairs Occasional Paper No. 60, 1981.

Sharron, H., 'Pulling the Town Hall to Pieces', *Guardian*, 5 December 1984.

Stephenson, H., 'Tories Tell Contractors to Use Sweated Labour', *New Statesman*, 9 December 1983.

Stewart, J., 'It's All About Control', *Community Care*, 5 March 1984.

Taylor-Gooby, P., 'The New Right and Social Policy', *Critical Social Policy*, Vol. 1, No. 1, 1981.

Taylor-Gooby, P., 'Two Cheers for the Welfare State: Public Opinion and Private Welfare', *Journal of Public Policy*, Vol. 2, Part 4, 1982.

Thatcher, M., *Let Our Children Grow Tall*, London: Centre for Policy Studies 1977.

Thatcher, M., 'Address to the WRVS National Conference', London: Conservative Party Central Office 1981.

Thatcher, M., Speech to the Conservative Party Conference, October 1982.

Thomas, D., 'Privatization and the Unions', *New Society*, 21 June 1984.

Thomas, H., 'Why the Task of Mrs Thatcher's Government Has Only Just Begun', *Guardian*, 30 May 1983.

Titmuss, R., *The Gift Relationship*, London: George Allen & Unwin 1970.

Tory Reform Group, *High Noon in the National Health Service*, London, 1984.

Townsend, D., 'Micawber's Lament', *New Society*, 19 April 1984.

Treasury, The, *The Government's Expenditure Plans 1985-86 to 1986-87*, Vol. II, London: Her Majesty's Stationery Office 1985.

TUC, *Contractors' Failures: The Privatization Experience*, London: 1984.

Tyrrell, Emmett Jr (ed), *The Future that Doesn't Work*, London: Doubleday 1977.

Unemployment Unit Briefing No. 6, February 1983.

Wade, D. and Picardie, J., 'Private Gain', *New Statesman*, 15 March 1983.

Walton, B., 'How to Save Education from Itself', *Times Higher Education Supplement*, 28 May 1982.

Walker, A., *et al*, 'Conservative Economic Policy: The Social Consequences', in Bull, D. and Wilding, P. (eds), *op. cit.*

Walker, M., 'Hissing All Their Mistery Lessons', *Guardian*, 20 June 1983.

Wapshott, N. and Brock, G., *Thatcher*, London: Futura 1983.

Webb, A. and Wistow, G., 'Over and Under', *Social Work Today*, 11 May 1982A.

Webb, A. and Wistow, G., 'The Rise Which Cuts', *New Society*, 23 September 1982B.

Wechsler, J., Introduction to Crawford, A., *The New Right and the Politics of Resentment*, New York: Pantheon 1980.

Weir, S., 'The Poverty Queue', *New Society*, 19 January 1984A.

Weir, S., 'Housing Nightmare', *New Society*, 27 January 1984B.

Whitfield, D., *Making It Public*, London: Pluto Press, 1983.

Wicks, M., 'The DHSS's Cold War Politics', *New Society*, 20 March 1980.

Wicks, M., 'Too Cold to Live', *Community Care*, 16 September 1982.

Williams, A., 'Where Crooks, Cheats and Tax Evaders are the Only Winners', *Guardian*, 4 November 1983.

Williams, R., 'The Rise of the Careerist Intelligentsia', *New Society*, 21 May 1981.

Wintour, P. and Wheen, F., 'The Knives Are Out', *New Statesman*, 15 October 1982.

Yeo, Tim, 'Our View' Editorial, Voluntary Action, April 1984.

Index